BRITAIN, 1750–1900

FOUNDATION EDITION

John D. Clare

Hodder & Stoughton
A MEMBER OF THE HODDER HEADLINE GROUP

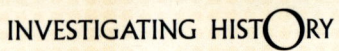

Acknowledgements

The publishers would like to thank the following individuals, institutions and companies for permission to reproduce copyright illustrations in this book:

Mary Evans: pp4, 6, 9 (l), 10 (b), 16, 22, 24, 29 (t and b), 32, 33, 47, 50, 68 (t), 69, 70, 73, 82; Punch: pp5, 66, 75, 84; Bridgeman Art Library: pp7, 10(t) (View of the Iron bridge, 1780 by William Williams (1740–1800) Ironbridge Gorge Museum, Telford, Shropshire, UK), 21 (Coalbrookdale by Night, 1808 (oil on canvas) by Philip James Loutherbourg (Jacques) de (1740–1812) Science Museum, London, UK), 39 (t) (Buckingham Palace: from St. James's Park, 1842 (litho) by Thomas Shotter Boys (1803–74) Guidhall Library, Corporation of London, UK), 40 (b) (Applicants for Admission to a Casual Ward, 1874 (oil on canvas) by Sir Samuel Luke Fildes (1844–1927) Royal Holloway), 41 (Hush! (The Concert) c. 1875 (oil on canvas) by James Jacques Tissot 91836-19020 Manchester Art Gallery, UK), 46 (Christ in the House of His Parents, 1863 (oil on canvas) by J. E. Millais (1829–96) & Solomon (1832–1886) Private Collection), 59 (The Election III The Polling, 1754–55 by William Hogarth (1697–1764) Courtesy of the Trustees of Sir John Soane's Museum, London), 65 (panel) by English School (18th century) Royal College of Surgeons, London, UK), 89; Topham Picturepoint: pp9 (r), 13, 30 (t, l), 40 (t), 49, 57, 90; CORBIS: pp11 (Jason Hawkes), 12 (© National Gallery Collection; By kind permission of the Trustees of the National Gallery, London), 14, 36 and 53 (Hulton-Deutsch Collection), 17 (t) and 55 (Historical Picture Archive), 39 (b) (Stapleton Collection), 78, 80–81 (Bojan Brecelj), 86 (Michael Masian Historic Photographs); British Museum, Department of prints and drawings: p19 (Cruikshank Tremendous Sacrifice Series); PA Photos: p23; Mansell/Timepix/Rex Features: p25; Manchester Public Libraries: pp27 (JR Barfoots: "Progress of Cotton" Plate 6 "Spinning"), p60; R.J Heald c/o Saltaire Tourist Information and Gift Centre Ltd, www.saltaire.yorks.com/touristinfo: pp30 (t; m and r) (b; l, m and l), 31 (all); Toledo Museum of Art: p35 (James Tissot (French, 1836–1902, London Visitors, 1874, oil on canvas, 63x 45 inches. (160 x 114.2cm) purchased with funds from the Libbey Endowment, Gift of Edward Drommond Libbey); AKG Photo: p38; Tate Gallery: pp43 (Henry Alexander Bowler (1824–1903) The Doubt: Can these Dry Bones Live? 1855 (oil on canvas)), 44 (William Holam Hunt (1827–1910) The Awakening of Conscience, 1853 (oil on canvas)), 67 (Sir Luke Fildes (1843–1927) The Doctor, 1891 (oil on canvas)); Hulton Getty: pp56, 71; Centre for the Study of Cartoons and Caricature, University of Kent, Canterbury, CT2 7NU: p62 (W.K. Haselden, Daily Mirror, 15 April, 1907); The British Museum: p68 (b) (© Bank of England); BoondocksNet.com: p77; Boston Irish Tourism Association: p83; British Library: pp87(#703/16), 88 (# 430/17 (33) © India Office); The Kobal Collection/20th Century Fox: p92.

Every effort has been made to trace and acknowledge ownership of copyright. The publishers will be glad to make suitable arrangements with any copyright holders whom it has not been possible to contact.

Note about the Internet links in the book. The user should be aware that URLs or web addresses change regularly. Every effort has been made to ensure the accuracy of the URLs provided in this book on going to press. It is inevitable, however, that some will change. It is sometimes possible to find a relocated web page, by just typing in the address of the home page for a website in the URL window of your browser.

Artworks by Chris Rothero (Beehive Illustration) and Richard Morris.

Orders: please contact Bookpoint Ltd, 130 Milton Park, Abingdon, Oxon OX14 4SB. Telephone: (44) 01235 827720. Fax: (44) 01235 400454. Lines are open from 9.00 - 6.00, Monday to Saturday, with a 24 hour message answering service. You can also order through our website www.hodderheadline.co.uk.

British Library Cataloguing in Publication Data
A catalogue record for this title is available from the British Library

ISBN 0 340 86909 7

First Published 2003
Impression number 10 9 8 7 6 5 4 3 2
Year 2009 2008 2007 2006 2005 2004

Copyright © John D. Clare 2003

All rights reserved. No part of this publication may be reproduced or transmitted in any form or by any means, electronic or mechanical, including photocopy, recording, or any information storage and retrieval system, without permission in writing from the publisher or under licence from the Copyright Licensing Agency Limited. Further details of such licences (for reprographic reproduction) may be obtained from the Copyright Licensing Agency Limited, of 90 Tottenham Court Road, London W1T 4LP.

Cover photo shows the painting: "Work" by Ford Maddox Brown 1863, courtesy of the Bridgeman Art Library.
Layout by Lorraine Inglis Design.
Originated by Dot Gradations Ltd, UK
Printed in Italy for Hodder & Stoughton Educational, a division of Hodder Headline, 338 Euston Road, London NW1 3BH

CONTENTS

Introduction
    What can Jack the Ripper tell us?   4

Chapter 1
    An Age of Wonder   7
    How did the Victorians feel about the Industrial Revolution?
    Pulling it together   18

Chapter 2
    A Case of Murder   19
    Did the Industrial Revolution destroy its own children?
    Pulling it together   34

Chapter 3
    A Tale of Two Cities   35
    What was life like in Dickens' London?
    Pulling it together   42

Chapter 4
    Victorian Religion   43
    Did God die in the nineteenth century?
    Pulling it together   52

Chapter 5
    Ruling Britannia   53
    Did the Victorians invent democracy?
    Pulling it together   64

Chapter 6
    Heroes in the Hunt for Health   65
    Who did most for medicine in the nineteenth century?
    Pulling it together   72

Chapter 7
    The Empire   73
    Should Britons be proud of the British Empire?
    Pulling it together   91

Postscript
    What did Jack the Ripper ever do for us?   92

Glossary   94
Index   96

INVESTIGATING HISTORY

INTRODUCTION
What can Jack the Ripper tell us?

SOURCE A

Whitechapel in 1870, a drawing by the Frenchman Gustav Doré.

> **THINK ABOUT IT**
>
> Look at Source A. Write a sentence each about:
> - the people
> - the street
> - what kind of place it seems to be.
>
> Try to use lots of colourful verbs and adjectives.

On 6 August 1888, a prostitute called Martha Tabram was murdered. On 31 August, Mary Ann Nichols was found dead. Then, on 8 September, another woman – 'Dark Annie' Chapman – was killed.

In all three murders, the killer had cut open the body. The police said the cuts might have been made by a doctor or a butcher.

Whitechapel in 1888 was a very poor place. About 40% of the 76,000 people living there did not have enough money to live. Half the people were poor Jews, and there were Irish, Russians, Poles and people from many other races. There were 1200 **prostitutes**.

On 30 September, two more prostitutes – Elizabeth Stride and Catherine Eddowes – were murdered and cut open within minutes of each other. The police found a note on a door saying 'The Jews did it', but they washed it off.

On 16 October, a letter and a bit of human kidney were sent to the police (see Source C). A month later another prostitute – Mary Kelly – was killed.

The police did not know who was doing the murders.

SOURCE B

Whitechapel

Nobody cares about life here. Down one street there is a cry of 'Murder'. A woman – her face slashed by a knife – runs out, chased by a madman. It is only a drunken husband having a row with his wife.

From a book about how poor people lived, written in 1889.

SOURCE C

Sir

I send you half the kidney I took from one of the women. The other half I cooked and ate. It was very nice. I might send you the knife.

Catch me if you can.

Letter sent to the police on 16 October 1888.

◆ The police could not tell if the letter came from the real killer, or if the kidney came from one of the murdered women.

SOURCE D

The London Police at that time did not know about fingerprints, blood types or any other of the modern ways we catch killers.

Written by a modern historian.

SOURCE E

BLIND-MAN'S BUFF.
(As played by the Police.)
"TURN ROUND THREE TIMES, AND CATCH WHOM YOU MAY!"

A cartoon from 1888. Did the cartoonist think the police were doing a good job of catching the killer?

THINK ABOUT IT

1. The police could not catch the killer. What reason does Source D give for this?
2. Source E suggests a different reason. What is it?

INVESTIGATING HISTORY

Everybody was talking about the murders. Even Queen Victoria said that the killer had to be found.

35 The police handed out 80,000 papers and questioned 2000 people. They talked to sailors, drug addicts, the cowboys from
40 a visiting Wild West show, and 76 butchers.

Many people said that the murders must have been done by someone who was mad.
45 Others agreed with Frederick Abberline, the policeman in charge, who thought that an Englishman could never have done such things, and that the murders
50 must have been done by a foreigner. The police named three main suspects – a mad doctor, a mad Pole, and a mad Russian doctor.

55 Some people, however, said that Whitechapel was to blame – it was so poor, so dirty and so overcrowded.

The poor people of Whitechapel
60 had other ideas. They said that the killer was a rich man. One suspect was Prince Albert Victor (Queen Victoria's grandson) who was known to hang round the gay
65 pubs of Whitechapel.

After Mary Kelly, the killer never struck again. Nobody has ever found out who did the murders.

The newspapers were full of the story.

THINK ABOUT IT

1. What does the story of Jack the Ripper tell us about:

   (a) What Victorians thought about poor people
   (b) What it was like to live in London.
   (c) What people thought about sex and religion.
   (d) The Queen and public opinion.
   (e) Doctors and the police.
   (f) What Victorians thought about foreigners.

2. How much had life in London changed since Tudor and Stuart times?

STOP AND REFLECT: Write six sentences to explain what the story of Jack the Ripper tells us about life in Britain in 1888.

CHAPTER 1

An Age of Wonder
How did the Victorians feel about the Industrial Revolution?

In this chapter you will:
- Find out how Britain changed during the Industrial Revolution.
- Study what the Victorians thought about the Industrial Revolution.
- Write an imaginary letter about the Great Exhibition.

SOURCE A

This picture, *Work*, was painted by Ford Madox Brown in 1863.
Can you see:
- the beer-seller, his eye hurt in a fight
- the little girl, whose parents are dead, acting as mother to her brothers and sisters
- rich people at the top of the painting, poor people at the bottom?

THINK ABOUT IT

1. Make a list of everything you can see happening in Source A.
2. Did the painter think that life in Victorian times was good?

INVESTIGATING HISTORY

Between 1750 and 1900 there was an '**Industrial Revolution**'. It began in Britain, and it made the world how it is today!

5 During this time, Britain became very rich and powerful, and built up an **Empire** that covered a fifth of the world.

The Victorians loved amazing things, and the more shocking, the better! They thought they were SO clever!

They thought that humankind was getting better and better every day, and that they were almost perfect!

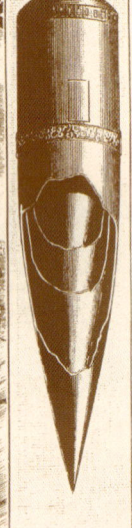

SOURCE B

This invention (1891) was for people who enjoyed being scared. The idea was that people would sit in the shell, which would then be dropped from the top of the Eiffel Tower.

The inventor was sure that the pool of water and the springs in the nose of the shell would stop the people being killed when they reached the ground at 172 miles per hour.

The idea was never tried.

SOURCE C

Progress

Young people today cannot know how much better life is for them than it was for me when I was young.

There were no gas lights, so at night I had to grope my way round London in the dark.

Because of the railways, I can go to London in six hours, faster than I used to be able to go to the next town.

Because of the police, I can walk round London without being attacked.

When it rained there were no umbrellas. There were no braces to hold up my underpants, and no painkillers when I was ill.

There were filthy coffee-houses, not the fine clubs of today. Parliament was useless and MPs took bribes. There were no banks to look after my money. And, however angry I got, there was no Post Office to take my letters anywhere in the world for a penny.

Yet, bad as things were, I lived on quietly, and I wasn't unhappy.

Reverend Sydney Smith (1771–1845).

◆ Reverend Sydney Smith thought the Industrial Revolution was not only making life better, but making PEOPLE better.

An Age of Wonder

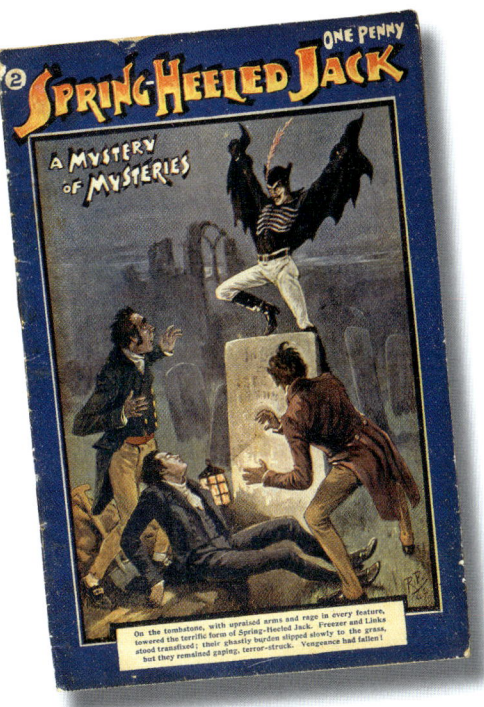

The Victorians thought that they were rich because they were better than other people. They said that ANYBODY can do well if they work hard. In the same way, the Victorians thought that Britain was the most powerful country because the British people were better than other races.

The flip-side of this was that the Victorians also thought that, if you were poor or powerless, it must be your own fault. They blamed drink and laziness for making poor people poor. They said that other races were stupid and uncivilised.

SOURCE D

Victorians loved scandal. They read cheap newspapers and trashy novels. They loved stories about nasty crimes and bad men.

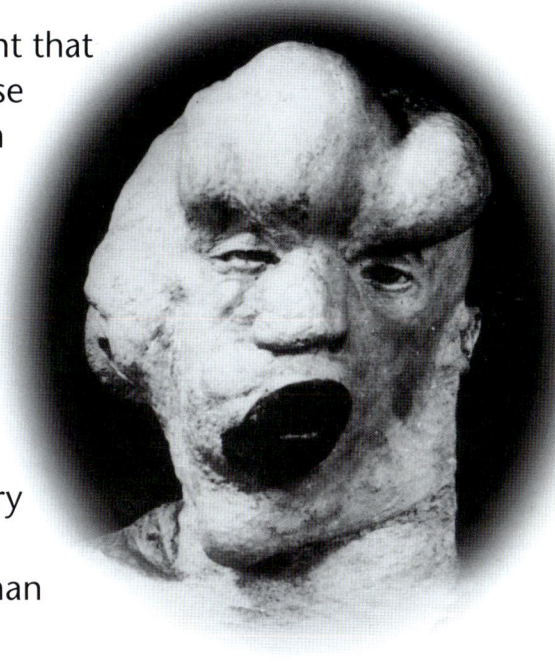

SOURCE E

Victorians loved 'Freak Shows'. One famous freak was John Merrick, the 'Elephant Man'. It was said that he looked so frightening that women ran away from him.

THINK ABOUT IT

1. Read Source C.
   - What EIGHT things had improved the writer's life?
   - For each thing, talk about *how* it would have made his life better.
   - List the words the writer uses to make things in the past sound bad.

2. Make a list of all the 'amazing things' mentioned on pages 7–9.

3. The Victorians loved wonders, but find some things on pages 7–9 that we would think *not* politically correct nowadays.

STOP AND REFLECT:
Finish these three sentences:
- The Victorians thought that they were rich and powerful because…
- They thought that the poor…
- They thought that other races…

9

How did the Industrial Revolution change industry?

SOURCE A

Ironbridge

We crossed the iron bridge and stopped there for half an hour. What can I say – it is one of the wonders of the world!

A visitor to Ironbridge in 1781.

Iron

In 1770, the iron industry was in trouble. Ironmakers used wood to make iron, and they could not get enough wood. So, they took up a discovery made by Abraham Darby in 1709 – they used coal to make iron. After 1770, there was a revolution in the iron industry.

People in Britain went iron mad. In 1781, Abraham Darby's grandson built the first iron bridge. The army used iron for cannons, the navy used it for ships. The new factories were made of iron, and so were the machines that were in them. Iron was used for trains and tools. In the home, it was used for fireplaces and cookers. One man built an iron church for his workers, and said he wanted to be buried in an iron coffin!

Iron became the basis of the Industrial Revolution.

Coal

Coal was used to power the steam engines used in factories and the railways. The Industrial Revolution could not have happened without coal.

Coal mining was a dangerous and dirty job. There were many pit disasters. It was said that 'Coal was King'. Britain's power was based on coal.

SOURCE B

This picture shows a disaster at a mine in County Durham in 1858. One newspaper sent an artist to every disaster to draw a picture of what had happened.

An Age of Wonder

Textiles

Before the Industrial Revolution, people made cloth by hand in their own homes.

After 1733, however, there were a number of inventions which meant that people could make cloth by machine. In fact, they could make it 200 times faster, and at a quarter of the price.

Because the new machines were too big to get into a house, people built factories to make cloth. And because the new machines were powered by steam engines, they built them on the coalfields in the north of England.

Many historians say that the changes in the textiles industry caused the Industrial Revolution.

SOURCE C

This mill in Bradford shows how much money was put into the textiles industry. One Victorian writer said that Britain's factories were 'greater in number, richer, more useful, and better-built than the useless buildings of the Egyptians and the Romans'.

FACT FILE

Industrial Revolution: Key Dates

- 1709 Abraham Darby made iron using coal.
- 1715 Newcomen developed a steam engine to drain the coalmines.
- 1733–79 Spinning inventions – helped the textile industries.
- 1781 Watt's steam engine.
- 1783 Henry Cort discovered a better way to make wrought iron.
- 1785 Cartwright's 'Power Loom' (steam-powered weaving).
- 1815 Safety Lamps (invented by Humphrey Davy and George Stephenson) helped coal-mining.
- 1856 Henry Bessemer (a way to mass-produce steel).

THINK ABOUT IT

1. Read pages 10–11. Think of as many words as you can that describe the Industrial Revolution, and choose the key FIVE.

2. Look at Sources A–C. If you had to choose ONE of these as the emblem of the Industrial Revolution, which would you choose, and why?

3. Find as many examples as you can of the iron, coal and textiles industries helping each other to grow.

STOP AND REFLECT: Write a sentence about what the Victorians thought about the Industrial Revolution.

INVESTIGATING HISTORY

How did railways change the Victorians' world?

Results of the railways

When the Victorians put together iron, coal and steam engines, they made... RAILWAYS!

Railways could carry more than any other kind of transport. They went faster and were cheaper than any other kind of transport. Railways could take you anywhere in Britain in less than a day. For the first time, people started to go to the seaside for their holidays.

Firms were set up to build the trains and the rails. The lines had to cross rivers, tunnel through hills and cross bogs. Railways paid out millions in wages and gave jobs to thousands of people.

In the past, every town had set its own clocks to 'about the right time'. Now, to stop trains crashing into each other, everybody had to set their watches to 'Railway Time'. Life everywhere speeded up. Railways changed the world.

SOURCE A

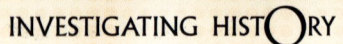

This picture, Rain, Steam and Speed by the English artist J M W Turner, shows a train crossing a bridge.
On the left, people sail on the river in a boat.

On the right, a man ploughs using horses. Through the middle of the painting crashes the train, modern, black, frightening, fire pouring from it.

12

An Age of Wonder

SOURCE B

The Railway Station by W P Frith (1862). Can you see:
- The station and the train?
- A thief being arrested?
- Mr Frith in the centre of the picture, with his family round him?
- A bride and groom?
- A boy off to school?

The picture was painted for a man called Louis Flatlow. At first, Mr Flatlow wanted to be shown driving the train, but the real driver would not let him, so in the end he had to settle for being shown just talking to the driver! Can you see him?

THINK ABOUT IT

1. What is the message of the painting *Rain, Steam and Speed*?

2. Imagine you are a Victorian from a small country village. You have just gone on a train for the first time, and you got off the train at Frith's Railway Station (Source B). With a partner, improvise a scene in which you tell your friend about what you saw and felt.

STOP AND REFLECT: Finish this sentence: 'J M W Turner thought that railways were...'

13

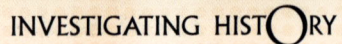
INVESTIGATING HISTORY

Was Brunel the 'Greatest Briton'?

In 2002, BBC2 TV asked people to vote for 'The Greatest Briton'. In the end, Winston Churchill came first, but in second place came Isambard Kingdom Brunel (1806–59). He got 400,000
5 votes – twice as many as Princess Diana! What was so great about Isambard Kingdom Brunel?

1. In 1823, when he was only 17, his father put him in charge of building a tunnel under the River Thames. It was a very difficult and dangerous job.

2. In 1829, aged just 23, Brunel planned the beautiful Clifton Bridge.

3. After 1831 (aged 25) he built the docks at many ports.

4. Brunel swallowed a penny that stuck in his lungs. When doctors could not get it out, Brunel invented a rocking table to get it out. It was used by doctors for many years after.

5. In 1833 (aged 27) Brunel became engineer of the Great Western Railway, said by many to be the best railway ever built.

6. Brunel worked 18 hours a day. Even when he took three days off for his honeymoon, he went to look at railways!

14

An Age of Wonder

7. In 1838 Brunel built the **Great Western**, the biggest steamboat ever built (70 metres long). In 1845 he built the **Great Britain** – the first big ship to be powered by a propeller.

8. He built a hospital for Florence Nightingale (1854).

9. In 1852, he began to build the **Great Eastern** – at the time, the biggest ship ever built. He had to overcome vast difficulties – there were problems building it, and he was attacked in the newspapers.

THINK ABOUT IT

1. Write an information text about Brunel for an encyclopaedia.
- Write clearly.
- Give facts, dates and numbers.
- Do not say what you feel about what he did.
- Tell the reader both good and bad things about Brunel.

2. Write a persuasion text about Brunel, trying to get people to agree that he was the greatest Briton.
- Use powerful adjectives that will make Brunel seem great.
- Enthuse about what he did.
- Only talk about the good things about him.

SOURCE B

Raving About Brunel

Isambard Kingdom Brunel took engineering to the top…

He gave everybody hope. People came to believe that humankind could do anything it wanted to do and go anywhere it wanted to go.

Written by a university professor.

STOP AND REFLECT: Write as much as you can to finish this sentence: 'Brunel was amazing because…'

What could you see at the Great Exhibition?

The Great Exhibition was held to show the rest of the world that Britain was the best, most powerful country.

It was opened on 1 May 1851 by Queen Victoria. More than six million people went to see it. There were more than 100,000 displays. There were displays about the world of nature, and on the history of art and building. There were thousands of displays showing the great wonders of modern industry.

If you went to the Great Exhibition, there were other things there too – bands played music, there was a circus, and you could go to see the biggest diamond in the world.

SOURCE A

Going into the building for the first time, you are amazed! There are displays from India, Africa, Canada, the West Indies…You can see Sheffield steel, wool and cloth, brass and iron, locks and grates, farm machinery and tools, coal and lead and iron, cotton machinery, rope-making machines, ship-engines and steam engines.

There are displays showing things from Persia, Greece, Egypt and Turkey. There are two big displays of cloth, weapons and machinery from France, and a display of farm machinery and wool from America.

In the British half you can see displays of fine cloth, jewellery, clocks, guns, chemicals, engineering, music, medicine, glass, knives and forks, farming, china and pottery, along with perfume, fishing, wax flowers and stained glass.

The Great Exhibition in 1851.

SOURCE B

The Crystal Palace, a huge glass building with an iron frame and 293,655 panes of glass. There had never been a building like it anywhere in the world.

An Age of Wonder

SOURCE C

The main hall of the Exhibition was 560 metres long and 124 metres wide.

The Exhibition was closed on Sundays, and the rules were no dogs, no smoking and no beer. Instead, more than a million
25 bottles of pop were sold.

SOURCE D

The British looked down on other races. In this cartoon, **cannibals** from the empire have their dinner at the café, but they are looking at the visitors' son!

THINK ABOUT IT

1. Using Source A, list all the different countries it mentions. How do you think it made the Victorians feel, when all those countries came to the Great Exhibition?

2. Everybody who saw the Great Exhibition was amazed. Can you explain why?

3. Why did the Victorians hold the Great Exhibition?

STOP AND REFLECT: Use pages 16–17 to make a list of all the things you might have seen at the Great Exhibition.

17

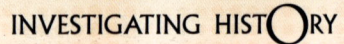

Pulling it Together

How did the Victorians feel about the Industrial Revolution?

This chapter has been about how amazing the Industrial Revolution was, and how amazed by it the Victorians were. The Victorians loved to be shocked and thrilled, and in this assignment you are going to pretend you are a Victorian, amazed and excited by the Great Exhibition.

Stage 1 Preparation

1. Look back at pages 7–17, and remind yourself of the kind of things that excited and thrilled the Victorians, and what the Victorians thought and said about them.

2. Get your list of 'things to see at the Great Exhibition'.

Stage 2 Writing the letter

Imagine that you are a Victorian visitor to the Great Exhibition, and write a letter to a friend about what you saw.

- Use 'I', and the past tense.

This is not just a simple recount text, part of your letter will be to persuade your friend that it was fantastic! So:

- Use evidence to back up what you are saying.
- Use a vocabulary of description, with lots of powerful adjectives such as 'huge' and 'stunning'.
- Describe scenes in dramatic language to help the reader build up a picture in his/her mind's eye.
- Include value judgements – saying what you felt and thought about what you saw. Try to make the reader agree with you.
- Sometimes, TELL the reader what to think.

> (a) *The basic letter* will describe what you 'saw' at the Exhibition – what the building looked like, and all the things that were there.
>
> (b) *A better letter* will use lots of different adjectives and verbs to say how thrilling and amazing it was.
>
> (c) *The very good letter* will explain what you 'saw' by linking it to what you know about the Industrial Revolution.
>
> (d) *The best letter* will include authentic Victorian attitudes.

CHAPTER 2
A Case of Murder
Did the Industrial Revolution destroy its own children?

In this chapter you will:
- **Find out whether the Victorians ruined the environment.**
- **Discuss whether workers were badly treated.**
- **Study how trade unions grew up in the nineteenth century.**
- **Decide whether the Industrial Revolution destroyed the people.**

Frederick Engels lived in Manchester. He was the son of a factory owner, but he hated the way poor people in Manchester had to live.

Engels said that the factories were to blame for the terrible lives of the poor. He said that people had become slaves of the machines. All their jobs were dull. And they were like slaves because they *had* to work because they *had* to get their wages to live.

In this cartoon from the time an evil factory owner is making cloth. He is making lots of money – but he is killing his workers.

But did the Industrial Revolution destroy people's lives? In fact, many Victorians really cared about the poor, and did a lot to help them.

But the Victorians loved to be shocked, and one way they did this was to go on about the *terrible* lives of the poor. Have historians been fooled by this into thinking that things were worse than they really were?

In this chapter, you are going to think about the effect that the Industrial Revolution had upon Britain and the British people. You will find out lots of ways that the Industrial Revolution killed people and destroyed their lives.

At the end, you are going to put the Industrial Revolution on trial for 'murder'. So, as you study this chapter, keep asking yourself – guilty or not guilty?

SOURCE B

The Industrial Revolution made the rich world we enjoy today, and paid for it with the blood of the workers — men, women and children.

Written by a modern historian.

FACT FILE
Victorian Reforms
1824 Workers could set up **trade unions**.
1833 The Factories Act improved work for children in factories.
1842 The Mines Act improved work for women and children in mines.
1847 The Ten Hours Act – women and children could only work 58 hours a week.
1908 **Pensions** for old people over 70.
1911 Sick pay for workers who were ill.

THINK ABOUT IT

1. Describe all the things you can see happening in Source A (page 19).
2. Talk as a class about the message of the cartoon, and how the cartoonist gets his point across.
3. Present the message the cartoon is making as a persuasion text.
   - Write, in your own words, the cartoon's message – that factories made money for the owners and clothes for the rich, but killed the workers to do so.
   - Use value-judgement words (like 'evil' and 'disgraceful') to influence the reader.

Did the Victorians ruin the environment?

SOURCE A

A painting of the iron works at Coalbrookdale. An Italian, who went there in 1787, said that going into Coalbrookdale was 'like going into hell.'

The Industrial Revolution damaged the countryside, and polluted the air and the rivers.

SOURCE B

The Iron Industry at Coalbrookdale

Coalbrook – you have been raped!

Among your grassy lanes and wild woods,

Your hills and wells, your rocks and streams,

Now we hear the heavy engines clang through the sweet valleys,

While many red fires with black flames shout on all the hills,

Turning the sun black with clouds of thick, smelly smoke,

That pollute the air, and blacken your clean waters.

A poem written by a woman in 1785.

THINK ABOUT IT

1. Study Source B. Find the words which show that the poet loved Coalbrookdale before industrialisation and that she hated the new ironworks.

2. Which tells you more about the effect that ironworks had on the environment – Source A or Source B?

INVESTIGATING HISTORY

SOURCE C

The 'Black Country' in the Midlands, in the Industrial Revolution. All over the north, factories poured out black smoke that turned the buildings black and destroyed people's lungs. The smoke went into the air – and caused the global warming that everybody is so worried about today.

At the time, people knew what was going on, and some people tried to stop the **pollution**. But nobody listened to them.

SOURCE D

Lead Poisoning of Lead Miners

A fit young man starts working in the mine, but after a few years he finds it hard to breathe. Also his spit is black when he is going home from work. He starts to eat less, and often sicks up the food he eats. He feels tired all the time, and has bad fits of coughing.

By the time he is 40 or 45, he is sick and tired, and has to give up work. He may last a few years more, but the poor worn-out miner soon dies.

A doctor who worked for a lead mine, telling the government about lead poisoning in 1864.

◆ Lead mining was a killer job – in 1858, the lead mining town of Alston had more widows than any other place in Britain.

◆ Textiles, coal mining and making matches were also high death-rate jobs.

SOURCE E

Bradford Canal in 1844

The drains of the town run into the canal. Also, the rubbish from all the factories falls into the water. The factory owners buy water from the owners of the canal. When they have used the water for their steam engines, they pump it – hot – back into the canal. So the canal is never cold, and the most awful gases and smells come from the water.

From a book about Bradford, written in 1881.

◆ The iron and chemical industries also damaged the rivers.

22

A Case of Murder

SOURCE F

On the coalfields, mines left huge pit heaps, like this one at Aberfan, in Wales. On 21 October 1966, it slid down onto the school, killing 144 people, 116 of them children.

SOURCE G

Britain was Damaged

When the Industrial Revolution was getting going, people did not understand about pollution. So the environment was damaged, and people fell sick.

But during the nineteenth century, the government began to do something to stop the pollution.

From a British government information sheet (1999).

FACT FILE
Victorians Laws against Pollution
1848 Act to make sure that rubbish was taken away.
1853 Act to stop smoke pollution.
1863 Act to stop chemicals polluting the rivers.
1865 Sewers Act.
1897 The **Public Health** Act – 'pure air, food, and water for all'.

THINK ABOUT IT

1. How is the Industrial Revolution still harming us, today?
2. If the Victorians did not know about pollution (Source G), can they be blamed for causing it?
3. If the Victorians tried to protect the environment (see Fact File), can we accuse them of *murdering* people (i.e. killing them on purpose)?
4. Can you think of any recent examples where firms have acted in a way that has led to death or damage to the environment?

STOP AND REFLECT: Write FOUR sentences on the effects of the Industrial Revolution on the air, the rivers, the countryside, and people's health.

23

INVESTIGATING HISTORY

Was there 'child-slavery' in the nineteenth century?

In 1830, a man called Richard Oastler said that the factory owners of Yorkshire were more cruel to their child workers than slave owners were to their slaves.

Was this fair? Let's find out…

SOURCE A

Factory children in the nineteenth century.

SOURCE B

What Historians have said about the Sadler Report

One of the most important ways for finding out about the kind of life led by the victims of the factories.

J L and B Hammond (1923).

One of the best sets of facts we have about what it was like in the factories.

B L Hutchins and A Harrison (1966).

Historians who want to find out what life was like for factory children in the Industrial Revolution usually use the *Parliamentary Report* of 1832, written by the MP Michael Sadler. This is what his report says.

Working in a factory

A child's day began at 4 a.m. The parents shook the children to wake them up (they had stayed awake all night so they would not sleep in).

The children had to run to the factory – sometimes two miles from their home. There was no time for breakfast. Some children tried to eat a bit of bread as they ran, and that was all they had until 12 noon.

If they were late – even half a minute – they were fined. Sometimes the **overlookers** would change the clocks to make sure they were late. The children were also fined for things like combing their hair, speaking, and opening a window. Overlookers who did not get a lot in fines were sacked.

Children started work as young as six years old. Because the overlookers would not let them sit down, their young bones bent, and gave them twisted spines, hunchbacks, knock knees and bow legs.

24

A Case of Murder

SOURCE C

A picture from the novel Michael Armstrong, Factory Boy *(1840). Can you see the girl sweeping up the cotton dust underneath the machine?*

Inside the cotton mill it was hot and damp. The machines were loud, which hurt the children's ears. The dust in the air got into
45 their lungs and made them ill, and got into their food and made them sick.

The children worked for 14 hours a day, with half an hour for lunch.
50 During busy times, one man said, they were made to work 19½ hours a day. During mealtimes, the children had to clean the machinery before they could eat.

55 As the children got tired, the overlookers would 'strap' them to make them work. Tired children would be thrown into a tub of water. One girl had an iron rod
60 pushed through her cheek, another child was strapped to death. One man told Sadler that you could always hear children crying in a factory.

Machines were dangerous, and 65 many children were killed. One man was pulled into a machine and killed. Another girl had her finger pulled off.

The children got home late at 70 night. They went to bed without eating. It was often midnight before they were in bed, and they had to be up at 4 a.m. to work next day. 75

One child told Sadler: 'I used to cry all the way as I went to the mill.'

THINK ABOUT IT

How did the artist in Source C make the factory seem a very sad and cruel place?

25

INVESTIGATING HIST*O*RY

SOURCE D

Interview with a Factory Child

At what age did you start work? Seven years old.

What was your job? Spinning.

How long did you work at that mill? From 5 a.m. till 8 p.m.

What time had you for meals? Half an hour at noon.

Had you no time for breakfast or refreshment in the afternoon? No, not one minute; we had to eat our meals as we could, standing.

You had $14\frac{1}{2}$ hours of work at 7 years of age? Yes.

What effect had this work on you? When I had worked about half a year, a weakness fell into my knees and my ankles became weak; and it has got worse.

Was it painful for you to move? Yes, in the morning I could not walk, and my brother and sister used to take me under each arm, and run with me to the mill, and my legs dragged on the ground. I could not walk because of the pain.

Were you sometimes late? Yes; and if we were five minutes late, the overlooker would take a strap, and hit us till we were black and blue.

Do you know of any accidents that happened? Yes, there was a boy who got hit by a machine, and he had both his legs broke, and from his knee to his hip the skin was ripped up as if it had been cut by a knife, his head was hurt, his eyes were nearly torn out, and his arms were broken.

Sadler Report, 1832: evidence of Joseph Hebergam

THINK ABOUT IT

1. Study Source D. Make a list of all the facts it gives about Joseph Hebergam's work in the factory.

2. Using all the information on pages 24–26, make up a set of questions and answers for an imaginary child worker, to imitate the actual interview of Joseph Hebergam.

3. Do you know of any countries today where children have to work in conditions like those in nineteenth-century Britain?

STOP AND REFLECT: Write as much as you can to finish this sentence: Factory work was horrid for children because...

Was Sadler correct?

Some historians do not believe the Sadler Report. They say he exaggerated, told lies, and put words into people's mouths.

A picture in a school book of 1835. Some people say that the artist of Source C used it for his picture of a cotton mill. If he did, the real thing does not seem anywhere near as cruel.

SOURCE F

Interview with a Factory Child's Father

At what time in the morning, in the brisk time, did those girls go to the mill? In the brisk time, for about six weeks, they have gone at 3 a.m., and ended at 10 p.m., or nearly half-past.

What time did they have for rest? Breakfast ¼ hour, and dinner ½ hour, and drinking ¼ hour.

How long did they sleep during those long hours? It was near 11 p.m. before we could get them into bed after getting a little food, and then my wife used to stop up all night, for fear that we could not get them ready for the time.

What time did you get them up in the morning? Me or my wife got up at 2 a.m. to dress them.

So that they had not above four hours' sleep at this time? No, they had not.

Were the children very tired by this labour? Many times; we have cried often when we have given them the little food we had to give them; we had to shake them, and they have fallen to sleep with the food in their mouths.

Sadler Report, 1832: evidence of Samuel Coulson.

THINK ABOUT IT

1. Study Source F.
   - Which answers seem to you to be exaggerated?
   - Which answers are just 'playing for sympathy'?
2. Now go back and look at Source D (page 26). Do any of Hebergam's answers seem exaggerated or playing for sympathy?

SOURCE G

Sadler wanted changes in the factories, and he used every dirty trick in the book – even telling lies.

Written by Lawrence Reed, a modern historian.

◆ Reed thinks that there are too many laws controlling factory owners today.

SOURCE H

Never has been printed such a mass of **biased** claims and downright lies.

Robert Hyde Greg (1837).

◆ Greg was a factory owner. Children worked at his factory.

SOURCE I

The Sadler Report was very biased. It was written by enemies of the factories. Sadler wanted to change the factories, so he was led into making lies. He asked people questions in such a way as to put answers into their mouths.

Frederick Engels (1844).

◆ Engels hated the factories.

Michael Sadler was leader of the MPs who wanted changes in the factories. In 1832, however, he lost his place in Parliament, and Lord Shaftesbury became the leader. In 1833, Shaftesbury made another report on children's work in the factories.

Shaftesbury said that the children did work long hours, and that there had to be laws to stop this. But he also found that Sadler's Report was exaggerated. Joseph Hebergam – who had told Sadler he had often been hurt at work – told Lord Shaftesbury: 'I meant things like hurting my fingers – nothing worse than that'.

THINK ABOUT IT

1. Look at Sources G–I attacking the Sadler report. Why is Source I the most powerful piece of evidence?

2. Engels (Source I) said that Sadler 'put answers into people's mouths'. Find examples in Sources D and F where Sadler did this.

A Case of Murder

SOURCE J

In the nineteenth century, some Victorians believed that the factories were GOOD for children – they gave them a wage, and let them eat!

After 1833, there were inspectors who went round the factories to make sure that child workers were treated well.

SOURCE L

Places of Fun

In the factory the machines do all the work. The children do almost nothing! It is lovely to see the clever way they do their little jobs for a short time, and to see them resting in between. I have never seen a child hit. They always seem happy and bright.

And I know that they do not get tired, because when they go out of the mill, they skip to the playground to play.

Written by Andrew Ure in 1835.

SOURCE K

A drawing of a girl working in a factory in 1884. She works 'half-time', and goes to school for the rest of the day.

THINK ABOUT IT

1. How are the pictures on pages 27–29 different from those on pages 24–25?

2. What would an historian who had only Sources J–L say about factory work?

3. Ask your teacher to lead a class discussion: 'Was Sadler telling the truth?'

STOP AND REFLECT: Write as much as you can to finish this sentence: I do not believe the Sadler Report because…

25

29

INVESTIGATING HISTORY

How was Saltaire a 'model village'?

By 1840 the wool town of Bradford was 'over-crowded, dirty and smoky'. One mill owner, Titus Salt, did not want his 3000 workers to have to
5   live there. So he built a lovely mill and village for them in the country, four miles outside Bradford.

Salt called his village 'Saltaire'. Children worked in his mill and he made his workers work very hard.   10
But he was a Christian, and he believed that he should use some of his money to give his workers happy lives.

(a) The mill (1853).   It was made of iron.   The chimney was 75 metres high, so the people would not be harmed by the smoke.

(b) The workmen's houses were well built.   The rents were low. The houses were not over-crowded, and Salt did not like mothers to have to go out to work.

(c) In 1854, Salt built a dining room, which sold cheap breakfasts and dinners.   He also built a bathhouse and a washhouse.

(d) When Salt's workers got old or sick, they could go and live in these '**almshouses**'.   They were given a little money, and the rent was free.

(e) In 1868, Salt opened a 6-bed hospital for his workers.   The workers gave a little money each week out of their wages for this.

(f) In 1868, Salt opened a school for 700 children – many of the children worked half-time at the mill.

A Case of Murder

(g) Salt built a night-school for his workers. There was no beer, but there were tea rooms, a library, a smoking room, a gym and school rooms.

(h) Across the road from the mill, Salt built this lovely church. He also built a Sunday School for 800 children.

THINK ABOUT IT

Using the facts on pages 30–31, write a guide book about Saltaire.

Write this as an information text:

- Start by writing about Titus Salt, who he was and what he did.
- Use headings to write about the different things.
- Address the reader as 'you' (e.g. 'If you go to… Can you see…')
- Give some facts, and try to be clear.
- As this will be for visitors, use some adjectives that say how lovely Saltaire is, and how great Titus Salt was.

(i) Bigger houses for the more important workers, such as the overlookers and two school teachers.

(j) In 1871, Salt opened a Park. It had gardens and a cricket ground, a boathouse, a cafe and a bandstand. But visitors could not spit, smoke, bet, drink beer or swear!

STOP AND REFLECT: Find evidence that Salt was not just trying to help his workers, but telling them how to live their lives.

31

How oppressed were workers in the nineteenth century?

In Britain today, most workers join a trade union. Trade unions try to get good wages for their members, and to make sure they are not
5 treated badly.

This has not always been so. Between 1799 and 1824 it was against the law to be in a trade union. Many farmers and factory
10 owners hated trade unions (can you think why?). Even after 1824 they stopped their workers joining a union.

The Tolpuddle Martyrs

George Loveless was a farm worker 15
in Dorset. In 1834, the local farmers gave the workers lower wages. So George and five other men set up a union.

Loveless made his friends swear an 20
oath to keep the union secret, but a local farmer – James Frampton – found out about it. Frampton knew of an old law that said it was wrong to swear an oath. 25

Loveless and his friends were put on trial (Frampton, his son and his step-brother were on the jury). They were sent to Australia for seven years. 30

Lots of people said that it was wrong to send the men to Australia. The government had to let them come back after four years.

Progress and failure 35

In the 1850s, strong unions were set up. In 1875, they won the right to **picket** – to stand outside a factory when they were on strike, to try to stop other workers 40
going in.

But these unions were only for skilled workers. For most workers, there was nothing.

The Tolpuddle Martyrs. Loveless is bottom right.

SOURCE A

The judge told people what to say… he told the jury that it would destroy the rich people if the workers could set up trade unions.

George Loveless, writing in 1839.

The match-girls' strike

In 1888, Annie Besant wrote about the Bryant and May match factory. Although the factory owner made lots of money, he only paid his girls four shillings a week. And he had many fines so he could take back even the little they got. He used an out-of-date way of making matches that gave the girls cancer of the face – called 'Phossy jaw'.

When they read this, Bryant and May were angry. They told their workers to sign a paper saying they were well-treated. Anybody who did not sign was sacked.

The girls were angry. All 1400 workers went on strike. They set up a union and asked Annie Besant to be their leader. They asked people to stop buying Bryant and May matches. After three weeks, they won! Bryant and May gave in, took back the women they had sacked, and stopped fining their workers.

After this, many other unskilled workers (such as the dockers) set up unions.

The match-girls' strike.

THINK ABOUT IT

1. Use pages 32–33 to draw up a Fact File about the trade unions.
2. Think about the stories of the Tolpuddle Martyrs and the match-girls' strike. Imagine you are either George Loveless or James Frampton, OR Annie Besant or Mr Bryant.

   Write three paragraphs about:
   - who you are and what you think about the situation
   - your opponents
   - why it will be a bad thing if you lose.

STOP AND REFLECT: Sum up what you have learned about trade unions by finishing this sentence:
'Overall, I think the workers were [well/badly] treated during the nineteenth century because…'

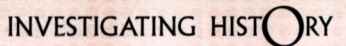

Pulling it Together

Did the Industrial Revolution destroy its own children?

- Some things you have learned about in this chapter have said: 'yes, it did'.
- Some things said: 'it didn't mean to do it'.
- Some things said: 'hey – that's an exaggeration!'

In this assignment, you are going to put the Industrial Revolution 'on trial'. Some pupils will try to persuade you that it was guilty of murder. Others will tell you that it was not guilty, or only guilty of manslaughter (unintentional killing).

Stage 1 Preparation

1. Divide into groups of five or six. Decide whether you are going to argue for the 'prosecution', or for the 'defence'.

2. Each group goes through pages 19–33, making a list of the names of witnesses you are going to call to give evidence (only choose people who will support your case, for instance, a prosecution group might decide to call Samuel Coulson, from page 27).

3. For each witness, make up a list of questions you will ask, together with the answers the witness would give (for instance, the prosecution might ask Coulson: 'What were conditions like for your children?' and his answer would include a description of their hours and punishments).

4. Ask your teacher to be the 'judge'.

Stage 2 The task

1. First the prosecution groups, then the defence groups, will call out witnesses and ask them questions.

2. The teacher and other pupils can ask them further questions, to see if they are lying or exaggerating.

3. Then the teacher will decide which side has won, and give grades to pupils according to how well they did.

(a) The basic case *will call witnesses who will tell people things that were bad (prosecution) or good (defence)*.

(b) A better case *will call witnesses who will give detailed answers*.

(c) The very good case *will explain how the facts prove the Industrial Revolution was (prosecution) or was not (defence) guilty of 'murder'*.

(d) The best case *will question the reliability of the witnesses*.

CHAPTER 3
A Tale of Two Cities
What was life like in Dickens' London?

In this chapter you will:
- Learn how Dickens wrote about London.
- Study pictures of London in the time of Dickens.

SOURCE A

This picture shows visitors going round London at 10.35 in the morning. Can you see the schoolboy who is showing them the sights?

Good and bad, rich and poor – towns in the nineteenth century had BOTH.

Towns built town halls, parks and swimming pools. They cleaned the streets and put in sewers. They had trams and fire engines.

But behind the lovely buildings and shop fronts were the nasty back streets and dirty houses of the poor. Even if you *could* go back in time to a poor place in London in the nineteenth century, you would not want to – the sights and smells would make you sick. It was as if there were two worlds, living side-by-side.

Charles Dickens lived in nineteenth-century London. When you read his books, you find out about these two worlds – rich and poor, nice and nasty.

What was it like to visit London in the time of Charles Dickens?

INVESTIGATING HISTORY

How did Charles Dickens write about London?

This picture shows the slums in which the poor people of London lived. Here is a list of problems they had:
- no clean water
- no **privies** (toilets)
- overflowing drains
- **middens** (muck-heaps) not removed
- raw sewage running in the streets
- diseases.

Rich people did not go to the poor areas of London.

SOURCE B

Dickens writes about a slum in Whitechapel – 'The Dials'

The stranger who finds himself in 'the Dials' will find lots around him to keep him interested for some time. From the square into which he has been plunged, the streets dart in every way, until they are lost in the nasty smell which hangs over the house-tops, and makes everything foggy and murky.

Lolling at every corner, as if they have left the narrow streets to come here to gasp for such fresh air as has been able to get this far, but is too tired to force its way up the streets, are groups of people, whose looks and homes would shock a normal person…

The visitor crosses streets of dirty houses, with now and then a little alley filled with houses as deformed as the half-naked children who play in the gutters. Here and there a pub, broken windows, plants which were planted when the Dials was built, in plant-pots as dirty as the Dials themselves, and shops to buy rags, bones and old iron, as dirty as the local bird-keepers and rabbit-sellers.

And everything lives together, with the pawn shops, which seem to have been put there by kind people as homes for fleas, together with posters for all kinds of things, and dirty men, filthy women, needy children, bad fruit, off fish, scrawny cats, sad dogs and thin hens.

Charles Dickens, Life in London (1835).

Dickens loved to write in great detail, using lots of words and making long lists of things. This was partly because in those days
5 writers wrote for cheap papers that came out every week and paid the writers so much a word. Dickens loved adjectives – sometimes he used new and odd
10 words in his writing.

Dickens sometimes read out his books to groups of ladies. So he wrote his books to be read out loud, and his words are often sing-
15 song and sound like poetry. Also, he filled his books with heart-breaking stories and sad people to make the ladies cry.

In his stories, Dickens would often
20 write about the people, the place and the weather in the same way, so that he built up the same 'feel' throughout the whole story.

SOURCE C

Poor Women Fruit and Vegetable Sellers

Such a stale, flat, thrown-out, cabbage-leaf and cabbage-stalk dress, such rotten-orange faces, such squashed pulp of people...

Charles Dickens, Our Mutual Friend *(1865).*

SOURCE D

A Boat Ride on the River

We went among the rows of ships, in and out, missing rusty chains and rotten ropes, pushing through wood chips, coal scum, in and out, hammers going in builders' yards, saws going at wood, clashing engines going at who-knows-what, ships going out to sea, and seamen shouting and swearing, in and out...

Charles Dickens, Great Expectations *(1861).*

THINK ABOUT IT

1. Read Sources B–D out loud two or three times each. Can you find times when Dickens:
   - makes long lists of details
   - repeats a phrase again and again
   - uses more than one adjective to describe something or someone
   - uses new or unusual adjectives
   - writes in a sad way about the needy state of poor people.
2. Study Source B. Explain how Dickens makes everything – the people, the place and even the air – sound dirty, tired and poor.

STOP AND REFLECT: 'His words are often sing-song and sound like poetry'. From Sources B–D, find a particularly poetic passage, and practise reading it out loud to a friend.

INVESTIGATING HIST**O**RY

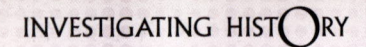

What might a tourist see in Dickens' London?

Study Sources E–J, which show scenes of London life about 1870.

SOURCE E

By 1900 there were 3000 buses carrying 500 million passengers a year. They were pulled by horses. Dickens loved going on a bus ride, seeing all the different people who got on and off. In this painting, you can see rich and poor people sharing the same bus, but can you see the look on the face of the woman with the red umbrella!

38

A Tale of Two Cities

SOURCE F

Every visitor to London has to go to Buckingham Palace. In Dickens' time, you could book to go round the palace gardens. Dickens did not like Buckingham Palace. He thought it was not grand enough to be the home of the Queen.

SOURCE G

Traffic jams were common in London – a survey in 1850 counted 1000 carts and buses passing in the streets every hour. There were 50,000 horses, which produced half a million tons of manure a year.

Dickens loved the busy streets, and thought they were like London's heart beating and pushing blood round its body. And there were all kinds of people there, too, including pick-pockets, drunks and beggars.

INVESTIGATING HISTORY

SOURCE H

Newgate Prison. Dickens came here in 1836, and was scared by the place and the people – as a child, his father had been put in prison, and Dickens had had to go and work in a factory. There were public hangings at Newgate until 1868.

SOURCE I

Poor people outside the **workhouse**, waiting to go in to sleep there for the night.
The Victorians thought the poor were poor because they were lazy and good-for-nothing. So they were very hard on them – the only place to get help was in the workhouse, where the poor people were made to break rocks.

40

A Tale of Two Cities

SOURCE J

Rich people had a lovely life. In the summer, they stayed in London for the dances and parties. In autumn they went to their country homes to shoot and hunt. Their life was 'eating, dancing, talking and flirting'.

This painting shows a ball in London in 1875. The host's daughter wants to play for the visitors, but they are too busy talking, so the painting is called 'Hush'.

THINK ABOUT IT

1. Study Sources E–J. Can you find examples where the poor were very poor and the rich were very rich.

2. Find a Source that shows a scene that you like, and which you think Dickens would have enjoyed writing about. Explain why you chose that picture.
   - List everything in the picture.
   - Using your list of things in the picture think of some exciting adjectives and verbs to describe them.

INVESTIGATING HISTORY

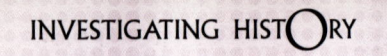

Pulling it Together

What was life like in Dickens' London?

Dickens loved – and hated – London! In one book, Dickens makes his hero David Copperfield say that London was 'full of wonders and wickedness'.

This assignment asks you to use your favourite picture from Sources E–J to write your own 'Dickens' passage, describing something you saw on a visit to London.

Stage 1 Preparation

1. Decide who 'you' are going to be – male or female, rich or poor, farmer or mill worker etc.

2. Re-read Sources B–D on pages 36–37, to remind yourself how Dickens wrote about things.

3. Look again at the Source you have chosen. Decide what effect ('feel') you are going to give to your description. Think of some adjectives that could be used to describe the people, place and weather to help you create this 'feel' throughout your passage.

Stage 2 The task

1. Write a recount of an imaginary visit to London, in the style of Charles Dickens, so it includes lots of facts and also plenty of description.

2. Start with an opening sentence saying how you came to the place, then describe it as enthusiastically as you can.

3. Remember when you are writing:

- Choose your words carefully to achieve the effect you want.
- Dickens uses long lists and repeats phrases
- Write about the poor in a very heart-breaking way.

4. Write a first draft, then read it to a friend. Read Sources B–D to remind yourself of Dickens' style of writing.

Work with your friend to make changes so that your piece sounds like Dickens.

(a) The basic account will tell a story of a trip to London, describing the place and the people.

(b) A better account will be detailed and lively, with lots of good adjectives and verbs.

(c) A very good account will draw out the contrast between rich and poor.

(d) The best account will reflect the style of Dickens.

CHAPTER 4

Victorian Religion
Did God die in the nineteenth century?

In this chapter you will:
- **Find out how important religion was in people's lives.**
- **Learn how Christianity was attacked in the nineteenth century.**

SOURCE A

This painting is called **The Doubt.** *A young woman wonders whether there is life after death. She is watching two butterflies, as she leans on a gravestone of a man called John Faithful. On the gravestone next to her the Latin word* **Resurgam** *means 'I shall rise'.*

In 1851, the government did a survey of religion in England.

It found that 7¼ million people had gone to church
5 that day – 40% of the population. At the time, people were disappointed at this – they wanted more people to go to church.

10 Some historians say that, during the nineteenth century, people in Britain turned away from the Church and religion. This chapter will
15 study whether they are right.

THINK ABOUT IT

1. What symbols of death can you see in the painting?
2. What symbols of life can you find?
3. What question is the painting asking, and what is its answer?

43

INVESTIGATING HISTORY

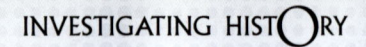

How important was religion in people's lives?

Religion filled people's lives:

- The vicar was an important landowner in the village.
- People had to give 10% of everything they produced to the Church.
- The Church ran the schools.
- Holy days were holidays, e.g. St Valentine's Day, Easter and Christmas.
- Dances etc. took place in the church hall.

SOURCE A

Holman Hunt, the painter, said that this painting was about the bible text: 'See your God'. It shows a woman who is sitting on the knee of her lover. She remembers a Sunday School song and stands up, wanting to change her life. The painting is full of religious symbols. Can you see:
- *The cat, playing with the bird (as the man is playing with her).*
- *The dropped glove (as the man will throw her away when he is bored).*
- *The flowers (a warning that good looks will fade).*
- *The painting over the fire (showing the bible story of a woman caught with her lover).*
- *A bright shaft of light (showing her sudden change of mind).*

Victorian Religion

SOURCE B

The Village Church

If the people in Lark Rise had been asked their religion, nine out of ten of them would have said 'Church of England', for all of them were baptised, married and buried there...

The church was full, for it was a tiny place. Inside it was as bare as a barn, with its grey, rough walls, plain-glass windows, and stone floor. The air was filled with the cold, damp, earthy smell of old churches with no heating. Sometimes there was a nasty sniff of something worse from the stacks of rotting bones under the floor....

The Squire's and vicar's families had pews at the front. Next to them were two long benches for the school-children. Below the steps was the little pedal organ, played by the vicar's daughter, and round it stood a choir of small school-girls. Then came the people, in their ranks, with the farmer's family in the front row, then the Squire's gardener and servants, the school teacher, and lastly the villagers, with the Church Warden at the back to keep order....

The service, with nothing left out, seemed to the children to go on for ever. But they did not dare to move; they sat in their stiff, stuffy, best clothes, full with their Sunday dinner, half asleep....

People who did not go to church led their lives by sayings such as 'Right is right and Wrong is no man's right'. They were all honest. And they were always quick to help anyone who was sad, or sick, or in trouble.

Flora Thompson, **Lark Rise** *(1939).*

◆ *Flora is describing her childhood in the 1880s in a small country village.*

THINK ABOUT IT

1. (a) Make a list from page 44 of all the ways that the Church affected people's lives.

   (b) Look carefully at Source A and then explain how religion had affected the woman's life. What effect did it have on the man?

2. (a) Look at Source B. How were the children of the village affected by the Church?

   (b) Make a list of all the adjectives in the second paragraph of Source B. What impression do they give us about the church at Lark Rise?

3. Explain using the third paragraph of Source B how the church helped to keep people in their place.

STOP AND REFLECT: Write as much as you can to finish this sentence:
'The most important way religion affected people's lives in the Victorian era was...'

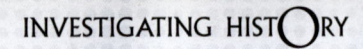

How was religion attacked in the nineteenth century?

This painting, Christ in the house of his parents (1850) upset Victorians because the floor of the workshop was dirty. People had never before thought of Jesus as an ordinary little boy who could cut his hand.

In Victorian Britain, Christianity was attacked from THREE sides:

1. New ideas about Religion

After the 1830s, new ideas about
5   Christianity came into Britain from Germany and France. They said that the Bible was not true. They said that Jesus was just an ordinary man, and that he did not rise from
10 the dead.

Nowadays, these ideas are nothing new. But the Victorians had never heard such things, and they were very upset and shocked by them.
15 Lots of people lost their faith in God.

SOURCE A

God Made the Earth

Heaven and earth were made together, at the same time. God made Man on the 23 October, 4004 BC, at 9 a.m.

Written by a Cambridge University professor in 1859.

SOURCE B

A 'Don't Know'

Bit by bit, I stopped believing in Christianity…

People had always told me that animals were so wonderful that they must have been made by God. But now I knew that animals had evolved to become like that slowly over millions of years.

I don't think we can ever know whether or not there is a God.

Charles Darwin, writing in 1880.

2. Communists

Communists such as Frederick Engels (see page 19) attacked Christianity because they said
20 religion was a trick to keep the poor people in their place. They said that religion stopped poor people trying to get a better life because they believed that things
25 would be better in heaven.

SOURCE C

This drawing mocks the idea that man had evolved from monkeys.

SOURCE D

If…

If man evolved from monkeys, religion is not true, laws are foolish, being good is a waste of time, **missionaries** are mad, and people are nothing but animals.

A university professor, writing in 1844.

THINK ABOUT IT

1. Write THREE sentences to explain how new ideas about religion, Communism and science harmed Christianity in the nineteenth century.

2. After more than a century of people putting their faith in science, are things better or worse than they used to be when people put their faith in God? Do we need religion in our lives today?

3. Science

The third thing that rocked Christianity was the idea of Charles Darwin (1859) that man had **evolved** from the apes.

Before Darwin, the Church had said that the fact that there was a world proved that there was a God – how else did we get here if God did not make us, it said? Darwin proved that there did not need to be a God to explain how we came to be here.

The Church attacked the new ideas. They laughed at Darwin (Source C) and said that his new ideas were evil (Source D). But they could not stop the new ideas.

Some people said that Darwin had proved that God did not exist. Many people began to say that people ought to put their faith in **Science**, not in religion – 'Love science, be scientific and you will become great', wrote one scientist.

STOP AND REFLECT: Write as much as you can to finish this sentence: 'In the nineteenth century, many people stopped believing in Christianity because…'

Victorian Religion

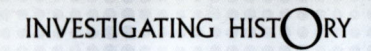

What evidence is there of faith in the nineteenth century?

Renewal

After 1833, people called 'High Churchmen' began to renew the Church of England. They rebuilt many churches. They put in flowers and candles, and wore lovely robes. They made their services more colourful, and many people in poor areas enjoyed them and started to go to church.

Revival

In 1859 there was a religious **revival** in Northern Ireland. The effects were so great that the courts closed because nobody did anything wrong, and the pubs shut because everybody stopped drinking.

There were many other revivals in the nineteenth century. The most successful was the visit by the Americans D L Moody and Ira D Sankey in 1873–5. They held big meetings, with singing and lively speeches.

Salvation

In 1878, William Booth set up the **Salvation Army** in the East End of London. Booth set up night shelters and food halls. By 1900 he had given out 27 million meals and 11 million homeless people had slept in his shelters. He set up a missing persons service and lent poor workers money to set them back on their feet. Women workers known as '**slum** sisters' went to live in poor areas, to help where they could, to talk about Jesus, and to show poor people how to live.

SOURCE A

A Revival in Wales in 1904

The meeting on Thursday night began at 7 o'clock and went on until 4.30 a.m. on Friday morning. During the whole time the people were keen and full of joy. There were about 400 people in the church when I went in about 9 o'clock.

I had not been there long when I realised that this was not like an ordinary church service. Nothing was written down. Instead, things happened when people felt like it. A young woman stood up and started off a **hymn** which everybody sang very loudly. While it was being sung, a few people fell to their knees and began crying for God to forgive them...

At 2.30 a.m., a well-known local person stood up and said that salvation had come to him. Everybody fell to their knees, and prayers went up from them all, while the preacher cried for joy. This went on for many minutes...

This account was written in a local newspaper, November 1904.

◆ In all, 100,000 became Christians in the Welsh revival in 1904.

Victorian Religion

SOURCE B

This Salvation Army picture is full of religious symbols. The drowning people are non-Christians going to hell. They 'see the light' and Christians 'save' them. 'The Rock' symbolises Christ.

William Booth wanted to take Christianity to the down-and-outs. They did not know any hymns, so he set Christian words to modern songs. He said: 'Why should the devil have all the best music?'

SOURCE C

There are all sorts of down-and-outs in the night shelter who have never been here before.

But there are also men who want to live a true and Godly life and see this is the way to get out of the hell that their lives have become. These men tell their friends how their lives have changed, and tell them that it is a good and happy thing to be saved by Jesus.

William Booth, writing in 1890.

THINK ABOUT IT

1. From Source A, make a list of all the evidence that the people there were fervently religious.

2. Make a list of all the ways William Booth tried to get down-and-outs to turn to God.

STOP AND REFLECT: Write notes in the form of five to ten bullet points which show that many people in the nineteenth century were religious.

What did missionaries do?

SOURCE A

God loved the world and sent His Son to save it. I love the world and I want it to be saved, and I am happy to die trying to do so.

The more I see of non-Christians, the more I hate the way they live. God! Help! Help! Save these poor people from slavery and the devil. Help them turn to Christ and live.

Said by David Livingstone.

SOURCE B

If Christ is not Lord of all, He is not Lord at all.

Said by James Hudson Taylor.

SOURCE C

In China, parents did not want a girl child. This drawing shows missionaries stopping parents killing a baby girl.

After 1850, many Christians became missionaries. They wanted to take Christianity to all the people of the world.

At the same time, they wanted to change the native people so that they adopted British ways.

By 1900 there were 61,000 missionaries all over the world.

There were more than 41 million Christians in Africa and Asia.

One bible mission had given out more than 203 million bibles.

One historian says that this proves that Christianity was still very much alive in the nineteenth century.

THINK ABOUT IT

1. Why did some Christians become missionaries?
2. Look at Source C. Did the Christians have any right to stop the Chinese people killing the baby?
3. From the Fact Files on page 51, find examples of missionaries:
   - healing people
   - setting up schools
   - stopping cruel customs
   - helping the people
   - trusting God
   - spreading Christianity.

MISSIONARIES FACT FILE

FACT FILE
James Hudson Taylor learned first aid and then went to China in 1858. He was told not to go inland, but he went anyway. He wore Chinese dress, so that the Chinese people might not be put off by his clothes.

He wrote the bible in Chinese and set up 205 missions stations with 849 missionaries. 125,000 Chinese people became Christians.

In 1870, his wife and two of his children died. He wrote: 'I am sad, but Jesus is my life and strength'.

FACT FILE
In 1876, aged 28, **Mary Slessor** went to Africa. The tribe she lived with believed that it was bad luck to have twins, so Mary spent most of her time trying to stop people killing them.

She wrote: 'War and the slave trade have almost stopped. People are not put to death when the king dies. There is less drunkenness. They want to go to school, and they want to live more civilised lives'.

FACT FILE
David Livingstone went to be a missionary in South Africa in 1841. Soon, he was going deep into Africa, trying to find new peoples to save. He walked all the way across Africa from from east to west.

Livingstone wrote: 'I do not want anything except Christ.' He hated the slave trade, and he tried to get it stopped.

FACT FILE
C T Studd was good at cricket, but he gave it up in 1885 to go as a missionary to China. He gave all his money away and trusted God to look after him.

In 1910, his doctor told him to stop work, so he went to be a missionary in Africa, where he died in 1931.

His last word was 'Hallelujah!'

FACT FILE
In 1794, **William Carey** went as a missionary to India. He wrote the bible in 30 different languages. He worked to help improve farming in India, and he stopped the custom of **Sutee** (where the wife of a dead man had to throw herself on the funeral fire and burn to death).

STOP AND REFLECT: From pages 50–51, write FIVE 'Amazing Facts about Missionaries'.

INVESTIGATING HISTORY

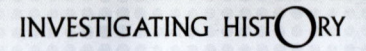

Pulling it Together

Did God die in the nineteenth century?

This chapter has looked at the problems faced by Christianity in the nineteenth century. Today, many firms ask for a 'SWOT' survey – a study of the firm's Strengths, Weaknesses, Opportunities and Threats. The 'strengths and weaknesses' look at how the firm is doing now; the 'opportunities and threats' are about what might happen in the future.

To do this assessment, you must imagine that you have been asked in 1900 to do a SWOT survey of Christianity.

Strengths	Weaknesses
• 41 million believers overseas	• New ideas from Germany and France
Opportunities	**Threats**

Stage 1 Preparation

1. Use the SWOT grid above.

2. Working with a group, look back through pages 43–51, writing onto the grid all the facts you can find to suggest that the Church was strong in the nineteenth century, and all the facts that show its weaknesses.
To help, I have put two ideas onto the grid.

3. Now, imagine that you are living in 1900. What might you hope would happen in the next century. Think of some ideas and write them down in the 'Opportunities' box. What would you fear might happen to religion? Write some ideas down in the 'Threats' box.

Stage 2 Making the presentation

Using the information on your grid, prepare a talk to give to the Archbishop of Canterbury, telling him the strengths, weaknesses, hopes and fears of religion in 1900.

(a) The basic presentation will tell him some facts about what people are doing and saying.

(b) A better presentation will have organised the facts properly into strengths, weaknesses, hopes and fears.

(c) A very good presentation will tell him the facts, but will explain WHY this is a strength or a weakness, an opportunity or a threat.

(d) The best presentation will be inventive and thought-provoking.

Ruling Britannia

CHAPTER 5

Ruling Britannia
Did the Victorians invent democracy?

In this chapter you will:
- Study how Britain moved towards democracy in the nineteenth century.
- Learn ways in which Britain was not very democratic.
- Talk about whether or not Britain was a democracy in 1914.

The Victorians believed that England was the happiest country in the world. Other countries like France were awful places – they were always having
5 revolutions.

The Victorians thought that Englishmen did not need a revolution because they were free men ruled by Parliament.

10 **Democracy** is 'government *by* the people, *for* the people'. Today, the government of Britain is a democracy. And the Victorians, too, thought
15 that their government was a democracy.

But were 'free-born Englishmen' so free? And was 'British democracy' as wonderful
20 as the Victorians thought?

In this drawing (1840) Queen Victoria is at the top, with the Houses of Parliament under her – and the workers under them all.

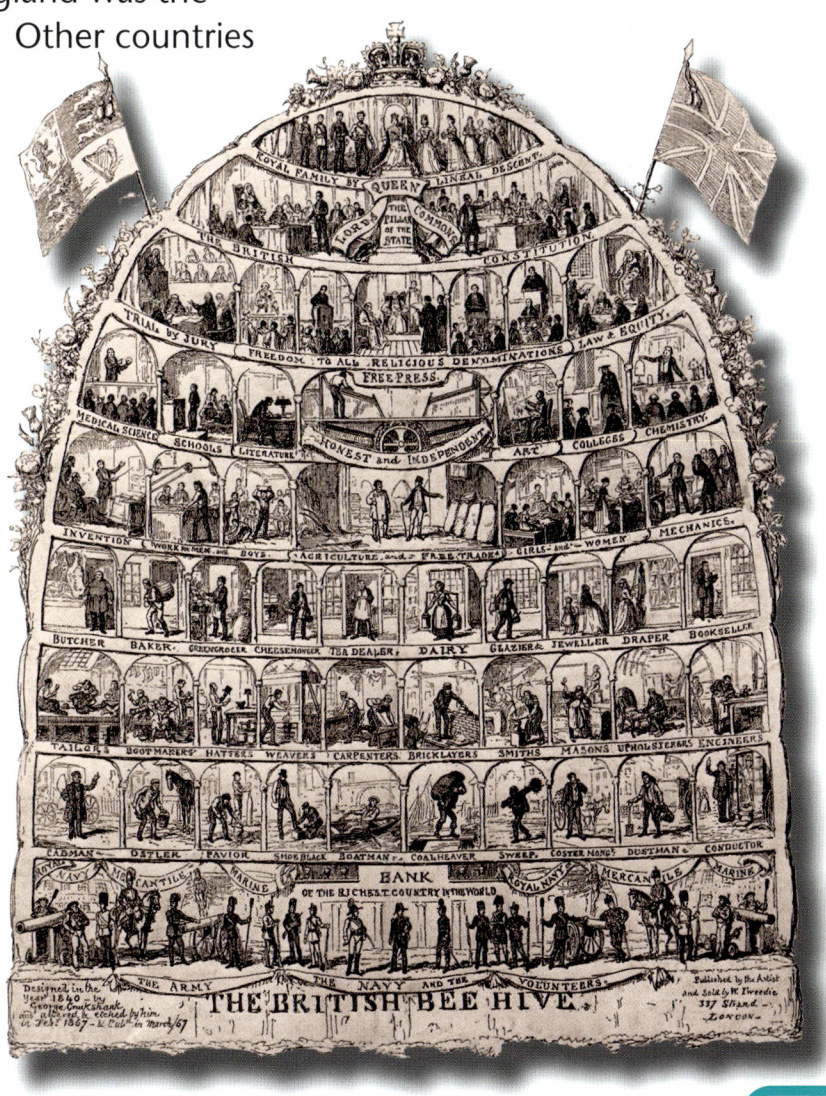

53

INVESTIGATING HISTORY

This chapter is split into two parts which disagree. The first part will try to tell you that the Victorians had a wonderful democracy. The second part will claim that Britain was far from democratic in the nineteenth century.

Your job will be to decide which side is telling the truth.

THINK ABOUT IT

1. Discuss, 'What is democracy'? Use these words: 'Parliament', 'free' and 'vote' in your answer.
2. From the Fact File, choose THREE events that seem very important. Explain your choice to the class.

FACT FILE

A Parliamentary Timeline

1688 The British Parliament chased out James II.

1715 George I of Hanover became king. There were two parties in Parliament, the Whigs and the Tories. An **election** had to be held every seven years.

1763 John Wilkes said the Prime Minister was telling lies.

1819 Peterloo massacre.

1832 The Great **Reform** Act. The Whig Party became 'the Liberal Party'.

1838 The **Chartists** presented the first *People's Charter* (they did so again in 1842 and 1848).

1858 People did not need to own land to be an MP.

1867 All male householders could vote.

1872 Voters could vote in secret.

1884 All British males over 21 could vote.

1885 **Constituencies** were changed so that they all had an equal number of voters.

1879–80 Midlothian election.

1892 Kier Hardie – first 'Labour' MP.

1893 Labour Party founded.

1897 Women started to ask for the vote (peacefully).

1900 The trade unions gave money to help the Labour Party.

1903 Women '**Suffragettes**' started to fight for votes for women.

1906 29 Labour Party MPs were elected to the House of Commons.

1911 The House of Commons reduced the power of the House of Lords. Elections every five years. MPs had to be paid.

1918 Women over 30 could vote.

1924 The First Labour government.

1928 Women over 21 could vote.

Argument One: YES!

The Prime Minister

In 1715, George I became king. George was a German. He did not speak English. He did not
5 rule the country himself. He left that to the most powerful man in Parliament, a man called Robert Walpole. Walpole was called the **Prime** (meaning 'most powerful')
10 **Minister**.

This is the way Britain is governed today.

Wilkes and liberty

John Wilkes was an MP. He was a
15 difficult and bad man. In 1763 Wilkes said that the Prime Minister was lying. He was put in prison.

Everybody was very angry. The people of Middlesex elected Wilkes
20 as their MP, even though the government tried to stop them.

This is why, in Britain, we have **freedom of speech** – the RIGHT to say that we think the
25 government is wrong.

This picture shows the House of Commons in 1808. People can watch the MPs as they talk. People from other countries said Britain's Parliament was the best government in the world.

Wilberforce and the abolition of the slave trade

William Wilberforce thought that it was wrong to sell slaves. Every year after 1788, Wilberforce asked Parliament to pass a law against it. 30

Lots of people helped Wilberforce. They went round the country trying to get people to support him. In the end Wilberforce won – Parliament **abolished** the slave trade in 1807. 35

It was the first time Parliament had passed a law *because the public wanted it.* 40

> **THINK ABOUT IT**
>
> Using page 55 only, make a list of facts about 'How Britain was governed in the eighteenth century' (e.g. there was a king).

Ruling Britannia

55

INVESTIGATING HISTORY

SOURCE A

A poster drawn by someone who wanted the reform of Parliament. At the top are the King and Lord Grey. The lion stands for the British people. At the bottom left, the Lords who do not want reform are running away.

The Great Reform Act, 1832

In 1830, Parliament was 565 years old! It was out of date. Some places that had been busy towns were just little villages. Some were no longer there at all! These places – called '**rotten boroughs**' – still sent two MPs to Parliament. Yet big new towns like Manchester had no MPs at all!

The Prime Minister (Lord Grey) and the House of Commons wanted to reform Parliament, the House of Lords did not. But the people wanted Parliament to change. In the end the King forced the House of Lords to agree to reform Parliament.

The Great Reform Act of 1832 stopped 56 rotten boroughs sending MPs to Parliament, and gave 63 MPs to towns in the north of England. It also gave the vote to anybody who owned land worth more than £100, which gave the vote to more people.

Some people say that the Reform Act of 1832 was the start of real democracy in Britain.

SOURCE B

The Reform Act of 1832 was the beginning of real democracy in Britain. The People had said what they wanted – that they wanted the country to be run by the House of Commons, and that they wanted the House of Commons to be elected by the people.

Written by a modern historian (1935).

THINK ABOUT IT

1. Look at Source A. Explain the message of the poster. How can we tell that the person who drew it supported the Reform Act?

2. Find FIVE facts on pages 56–57 to support the idea that 'The Reform Act of 1832 was the beginning of real democracy in Britain'.

3. Write as much as you can to finish this sentence: 'The Great Reform Act of 1832 was important because…'

Benefits to the people

After 1832, Parliament began to pass laws that would make people happy. They passed Acts to stop young children working in the factories and mines, and to stop factory owners making people work long hours. They passed laws to make bread cheaper and to improve public health.

More reforms

In 1867, the Second Reform Act gave the vote to every man who had a house, and in 1884 the Third Reform Act gave the vote to every British man who was not mad, a criminal, or a lord.

In 1872, the **Ballot** Act said that people had to vote in secret, by putting their ballot paper in a ballot box. This stopped people bribing or bullying voters into voting for them.

Government for the people

Government BY the people led to laws FOR the people.

- Children had to go to school (1870).
- Old age pensions (1908).
- Sick pay for workers who became ill, and **dole** money for people who lost their jobs ('the People's Budget', 1910).

SOURCE C

In 1910, the House of Lords tried to stop the People's Budget. So in 1911, the House of Commons passed the Parliament Act which said that the House of Lords has to agree to the laws passed by the House of Commons.

THINK ABOUT IT

1. Explain why the Ballot Act 'stopped people paying or bullying voters into voting for them'.
2. Which side did the artist of Source C support in 1910, the People or the House of Lords? How can you tell?

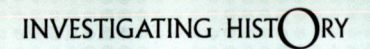

The Midlothian Campaign

Because ordinary men now had the vote, MPs had to change the way they tried to get votes. In 1879–80, in Scotland, the Prime Minister William Gladstone copied the revival meetings, starting his meetings with songs, and giving lively speeches. Newspapermen were asked to go, so other people could read in the newspapers what he said.

The rise of the Labour Party

After 1884, ordinary working men had the vote. They wanted MPs in Parliament who would stick up for them. In 1892, a Scottish trade union leader called Kier Hardie was elected as MP for West Ham in London. He was the first 'Labour' MP.

In Bradford in 1893, the 'Labour Party' was formed. The trade unions gave it money and 29 Labour MPs were elected to the House of Commons in 1906.

After 1911, MPs were paid, which let poor people become MPs. The Labour Party grew quickly.

In 1924, for the first time, there was a Labour government in Britain.

SOURCE D

Getting Labour Voters

In the early days, many young preachers joined the Labour Party because they believed that it would help ordinary people. It was like a religion. They got on their bikes and went to the villages. They sang songs to get a crowd round them, and then gave talks about the Labour Party. They stuck posters all over – sometimes even on the cows – saying 'Workers of the World Unite!'

Philip Snowden, remembering in 1934.

◆ *Snowden was one of these young men. In the villages he told people to 'come to Labour', just as in church he told them to 'come to Jesus'.*

THINK ABOUT IT

Study Source D.

1. Why did the young Labour supporters stick posters on cows?
2. Find TWO ways the early Labour Party was 'like a religion'.
3. Suggest reasons *why* the early Labour Party was 'like a religion'.

STOP AND REFLECT: From pages 55–58, make a list of TEN facts to support the idea that Britain had a wonderful democracy by 1900.

Argument Two: NO!

The frightening thing about Source E is that it really happened – in Oxford in 1754! Britain in the eighteenth century was NOT a democracy.

- Before 1832 there were only 450,000 voters out of a population of $6\frac{1}{2}$ million people.
- Some places (called 'rotten boroughs') had only a handful of voters – so rich people could buy and bribe their way into Parliament.
- In some places (called '**pocket boroughs**'), the landowner was the ONLY voter, so he sent to Parliament whoever he wanted.
- In Parliament, MPs sold their votes for easy government jobs, or for money.

Nobody cared what 'the People' wanted.

SOURCE E

This painting shows voters voting in the eighteenth century. One of the voters does not understand what is happening – the man behind is telling him how to vote. Behind them, two thugs drag a dying man to give his vote. All of the voters have been bribed.

INVESTIGATING HISTORY

Bad government

Until 1832, the government was run by lords and rich people. They did nothing to help ordinary people. In the 1790s, poor people were left to die of hunger.

And when there was a revolution in France in 1789, the government banned trade unions, threw people into prison without a trial, and used spies to trick people into breaking the law. Nowadays, we protest about countries where that sort of thing happens.

Peterloo

In 1819, there was a big meeting at St Peter's Field in Manchester to call for the Reform of Parliament. 50,000 people went — many people took their children. NOBODY wanted trouble. As soon as the speaker began his talk, the crowd was attacked by soldiers. Fifteen people died at 'Peterloo', as it was called.

One of the people put in prison after Peterloo was the reporter from **The Times**, *who was only there to write about the meeting. When* **The Times** *said this was wrong, the government passed a law to stop newspapers saying anything bad about the government.*

SOURCE F

Reform Parliament!

It is the work of the workers that makes this country rich, yet the rich people call you 'the Rabble', 'the Mob', 'the scum of the earth'…

The answer is a Reform of the House of Commons — sometimes called 'the People's House of Parliament'.

William Cobbett, writing in 1816.

◆ *Some people at the time could see that the government was rotten, and that Britain was not a democracy.*

THINK ABOUT IT

1. Rewrite Source F in your own words.

2. From pages 59–60, find FIVE 'things that were wrong' about the government.

3. Imagine it is 1831. Write a persuasive text: 'Things must change!'

   - Start by saying that Britain is not a democracy then say what is wrong.
   - Use emotive words to influence your readers.
   - Give facts and examples to prove what you are saying.
   - Repeat one powerful phrase (e.g. 'this is WRONG!') throughout the passage.
   - Finish with a good sentence calling for the reform of Parliament.

Ruling Britannia

The Chartists

There was a reform of Parliament in 1832, but it did not give the vote to ordinary people. Only rich people could vote, and only rich people became MPs.

In 1838 a group of working people got together to try to get the vote for ordinary men. They were called the 'Chartists' because they asked the government to agree to a 'People's Charter' (see Source G). They got 1,200,000 people to sign the Charter, but when they took it to Parliament in 1839, the MPs ignored it. There was a small rebellion in Wales in 1839, but it was put down.

The Chartists tried again in 1842 and 1848, but both times Parliament would have nothing to do with them.

Britain was a long way from being a democracy in the nineteenth century. In fact, few people in Britain wanted democracy. They believed that the rich people *ought* to rule the country.

FACT FILE
The Number of Voters

Date	No. Voters	No. Adults	%age
1830	450,000	6½ million	7
1832	650,000	6½ million	10
1867	2,000,000	10 million	20
1884	5,000,000	11 million	45

SOURCE G

The Chartists' Demands

1. The vote for all men over 21.
2. A new Parliament every year.
3. Vote by secret ballot.
4. Constituencies of equal size.
5. MPs do not have to be landowners.
6. MPs should be paid.

From the 1838 Charter.

◆ Using the Fact File on page 54, find out how many of the things the Chartists wanted were given in the end.

SOURCE H

What Labour Wants

To the voters

- Your vote can get Labour MPs into Parliament.
- The House of Commons is called 'the People's House', but 'the People' are not there.
- Nobody is caring for the old people. There is bad housing. Children still go hungry.
- You can make sure that Parliament does what YOU want.

Vote Labour

What Labour wanted in 1906.

THINK ABOUT IT

1. Look at Source G. Which, do you think, is the most important demand? Why?
2. How is Source H like Source F?

INVESTIGATING HISTORY

SOURCE 1

This cartoon – its title is 'Revolt of the Dove' – was drawn in 1907. In the top left ('once upon a time') the wife obeys her husband. Now she is telling her husband what to do and bullying him.

Votes for women

Until 1884, a Victorian wife belonged to her husband. She had to look after him and do as he said. In 1900, women did not have the right to vote.

Not only did many men think women should not have the vote, many women thought so too!

So, in 1903, Emmeline Pankhurst formed the 'Suffragettes' to try to get the vote. What made the Suffragettes different was that they fought to get the vote.

But the Suffragettes failed. Their tactics (see Fact File) turned people against them. When the First World War broke out in 1914, women STILL did not have the vote.

Ruling Britannia

SOURCE J

Why Women Should Not Have The Vote

I believe that – if women became MPs – Parliament would change. I think all men will agree that they cannot talk openly when women are in the room. It is very different to how men behave when they are talking freely with other men.

The way the Suffragettes have acted in the last year or two tells us that women are not fit to become MPs… It seems to me that, if we give the vote to women, the women who become MPs will not be the quiet, clever, good women. They will be those awful women who have made women look so bad. It would wreck Parliament…

It is not cricket for women to use force… In fact, it makes me feel sick when women use force.

Where are the women traders and the women bankers? Where are the important women who run the world? Nowhere do we see a woman in charge of anything. It seems to me that it is one of the truths on which **civilisation** is built that it is MEN who have to run the country. To start to let women run the country would be a very frightening and dangerous experiment.

I believe that normal men and normal women agree that men should be the boss. Women do not like a man who behaves like a girl, and men do not like a manly woman – which shows that this is true.

Viscount Helmsley, speaking in Parliament in 1912.

◆ Women over 30 did not get the vote until 1918, and women over 21 not until 1928.

FACT FILE
Tactics of the Suffragettes
- Broke shop windows.
- Chained themselves to railings.
- Went to 10 Downing Street.
- Went to the House of Commons and shouted at MPs.
- Burned down churches.
- Attacked policemen.
- When they were put in prison, they went on hunger strike.
- In 1913, Emily Davison threw herself under the king's horse in a horse race.

THINK ABOUT IT

1. Read Source J. Explain the FOUR reasons given by Helmsley why women should not have the vote.

2. From page 62, find TWO more reasons why men thought women should not have the vote.

STOP AND REFLECT: From pages 55–58, make a list of TEN facts to support the idea that Britain did not have a wonderful democracy by 1900.

INVESTIGATING HISTORY

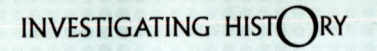

Pulling it Together

Did the Victorians invent democracy?

The issue of this chapter has been to think whether Britain's government in the nineteenth century was a wonderful democracy.

Some historians say that Britain became a democracy in 1832, and that Britain gave democracy to the world.

BUT
Lots of people say that Britain was not a democracy until 1928 (and that America gave democracy to the world).

Your task is to decide what you think – was Britain a 'democracy' in the nineteenth century?

Stage 1 Preparation

1. Work with a friend.

- One of you looks back over pages 55–58 and makes a list of all the good things about Britain's government in the nineteenth century.

- The other looks back over pages 59–63 and makes a list of bad things.

2. Share your findings.

3. Have a class debate – was Britain a 'democracy' in the nineteenth century?

Stage 2 Writing it down

1. In your first paragraph write as much as you can to finish off this sentence starter:

'There were lots of good things about the British government in the nineteenth century…

2. In the second paragraph, finish off this sentence:
'There were also lots of bad things about Britain's government in the nineteenth century…'

3. Finish with a conclusion in which you start: 'Overall, I think that…'

(a) A basic presentation *will give some facts about Britain's government in the nineteenth century.*

(b) A better presentation *will explain some of the good and bad things about the government.*

(c) A very good presentation *will go beyond 'good' and 'bad' and will explain whether things were democratic or undemocratic.*

(d) The best presentation *will evaluate whether the government deserves to be called a democracy.*

CHAPTER 6

Heroes in the Hunt for Health

Who did the most for medicine in the nineteenth century?

SOURCE A

An operation to amputate a leg about 1800. Today, a doctor doing an operation like this would be put in prison.

SOURCE B

A Deadly Operation

Cut off the leg in 2½ minutes (the man died later of blood poisoning). Cut off the fingers of the nurse (who died later of blood poisoning). Also slashed through the coat of a man who was watching, who dropped dead of fright. It was the only operation in history where THREE people died!

Written by a modern historian.

◆ In the days before pain-killers, doctors had to work quickly.

◆ The doctor in this story died in 1847 after he cut his own finger, and died of blood-poisoning.

In this chapter you will:
- Find out what was wrong with medicine in 1800.
- Study the work of 6 great people to improve medicine.
- Write a webpage about the person who did most to improve health.

Until 1800, doctors killed more people than they cured.

In this chapter you will find out about the people who improved medicine. If you have ever been ill, you need to say thank you to these people. Without them, you would probably be dead.

THINK ABOUT IT

Make a list of things in Source A that would not happen at an operation nowadays.

65

INVESTIGATING HISTORY

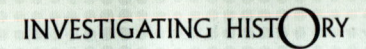

What were doctors like in 1800?

Medical care in 1800

Doctors could do operations very quickly. But the people often died afterwards, of blood poisoning, or of bleeding, or of the pain.

5   Also, doctors did not know about germs. So they could not cure anybody. Their 'cures' often stopped people getting better, e.g. they put leeches all over them to suck their blood! More women died after having a baby in
10 hospital than died in London's dirtiest houses.

SOURCE D

Where the Germs Came From

The doctor used to do his operations in a dirty old coat, covered in blood and spotted with pus… An old nurse, who had worked all her life in the hospital, said to me: 'I do not think the doctors do much good, and I think operations do more harm than good.'

London hospitals in 1871.

THINK ABOUT IT

1. What does Source C tell us about doctors in the nineteenth century?
2. Compare the doctors in Sources C and E. Which doctor had more chance of curing the patient?

SOURCE C

In this cartoon from 1869, a doctor tells a pretty woman to take some nasty medicine. When she says she does not want to, he tells her to drink a sweet wine instead!

Heroes in the Hunt for Health

SOURCE E

In this 1890 painting, **The Doctor,** *by Sir Luke Fildes, a child is very ill. There is a bottle of medicine on the table, but the doctor is looking at the child. The parents watch. It is dawn. The painter's eldest son had died in 1877, and Fildes painted this because the doctor had shown so much care for his son.*

THINK ABOUT IT

1. Study Source E.
   - List everything you can see in the picture.
   - What is the message of the picture?
   - Why did the painter paint it?

2. Imagine you are the mother in Source E. Write a letter to your sister telling her about your child's illness, and about what the doctor did.

   In this letter you will use:
   - first person past tense
   - connectives related to time (e.g. 'then')
   - powerful words for this sad event.

   Is your child going to live or die?

STOP AND REFLECT: Write as much as you can to finish this sentence: 'Medicine in 1800 was no good because...'

67

Who were the heroes of health?

Medicine improved in the nineteenth century. Here you will learn about the people who helped it do so – your job is to see who you think was the most important.

1. Before 1800, doctors had no way to stop pain. Imagine having a leg cut off without painkillers! One doctor, **James Simpson**, found it so difficult to watch that he almost stopped being a doctor.

So, in 1847, he discovered chloroform. In 1853, Queen Victoria took chloroform to stop the pain of having a baby.

Operations stopped being so terrible. Doctors could work more slowly and carefully. And there was no pain. In 1865, the French gave Simpson a medal for giving the greatest gift to humankind.

SOURCE F

Thank God for Chloroform

Dear Mr Simpson

Before painkillers, a man going to an operation was like a man going to be killed. Many people died rather than have the operation that would save their life…

When I first heard that you had discovered a painkiller I could not believe it. I thank God for giving you the idea to find a way to stop pain.

Yours truly

An old man

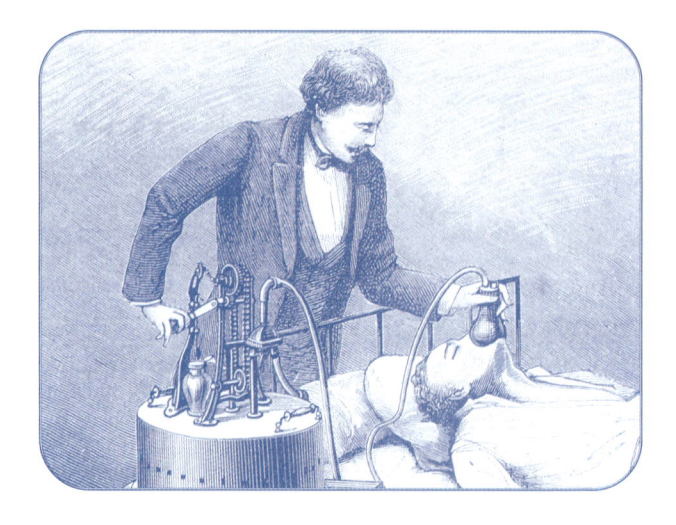

2. **Florence Nightingale** wanted to be a nurse, but her father would not let her – in those days, only the poorest, dirtiest women went to be nurses.

In 1854, Florence took some nurses to help in the war in Russia. Before she went, many wounded soldiers died. She cleaned up the hospital and the soldiers started to get better.

When she came back to Britain, she was so tired and ill that she never got out of bed again. But, even so, she set up the Nightingale School for Nurses (1859). She made sure that Britain's hospitals had good nurses.

Florence Nightingale – the only one of our 'heroes' to get her picture on our money!

Heroes in the Hunt for Health

3. **Edwin Chadwick** was an expert on the Poor Law. But he could see that many people became poor when they became ill. He got the government to pass the first Public Health Act (1848) forcing towns to build sewers, clean the streets and improve housing.

Chadwick was not a nice man and Parliament soon sacked him. But can you imagine living in a town *without* laws about public health?

> **FACT FILE**
>
> **Historians have said that Chadwick:**
> - got people to see that they needed public health
> - got the government to see that it ought to do something
> - was the first person to collect facts and figures about public health
> - invented a new kind of sewer
> - said that you cannot just dump sewage in rivers.
>
> One historian said Chadwick saved more lives than all the doctors put together.

4. **Louis Pasteur**'s daughter became ill and died. This is why he wanted to know why people became ill. He discovered that germs caused disease.

This idea changed medicine. Doctors knew that, if they could kill the germs, they could cure the disease. The germ theory of disease also led to Joseph Lister's work on **antiseptics** (see page 70).

In 1880, Pasteur and his team were working on a disease that killed chicken. They were giving chickens the disease. One day, they used some old germs to make the chickens ill – and the chickens got better! Pasteur had discovered **inoculation**. Today, when you have your BCG, you owe it – and your health – to Louis Pasteur, who wanted to stop you dying as his daughter had done.

> **FACT FILE**
>
> **What historians have said about Pasteur**
> - 'If we were looking for the greatest people in the world, Louis Pasteur would be one of them.'
> - 'The "germ theory of disease" is the most important idea in the history of medicine. It is the basis of everything doctors do today.'
> - 'There is no more important discovery in the history of mankind.'

Pasteur at work.

5. **Joseph Lister** was a doctor in Glasgow.   Although at that time operations were painless, half the patients still died after an operation.

Lister thought that dirt had something to do with this.   He tried keeping the hospital clean but people still died.

Then, in 1865, he read about Pasteur's germ theory of disease.   He started to use antiseptics to kill the germs.

It worked.   From that time on, none of Lister's patients died of blood poisoning.

At first, doctors mocked Lister.   But antiseptics worked, and they had to change.

Lister's discovery was a turning point.   The history of medicine is split into 'before Lister' and 'after Lister'.   Before Lister, patients usually died after an operation.   Now, they lived.

For the first time, doctors dared to do operations inside the body.   In 1896, the first heart operation was carried out.

In 1892, at a meeting to give Louis Pasteur a medal, Pasteur turned to Lister and said: 'there is the man who has done most to heal humankind'.

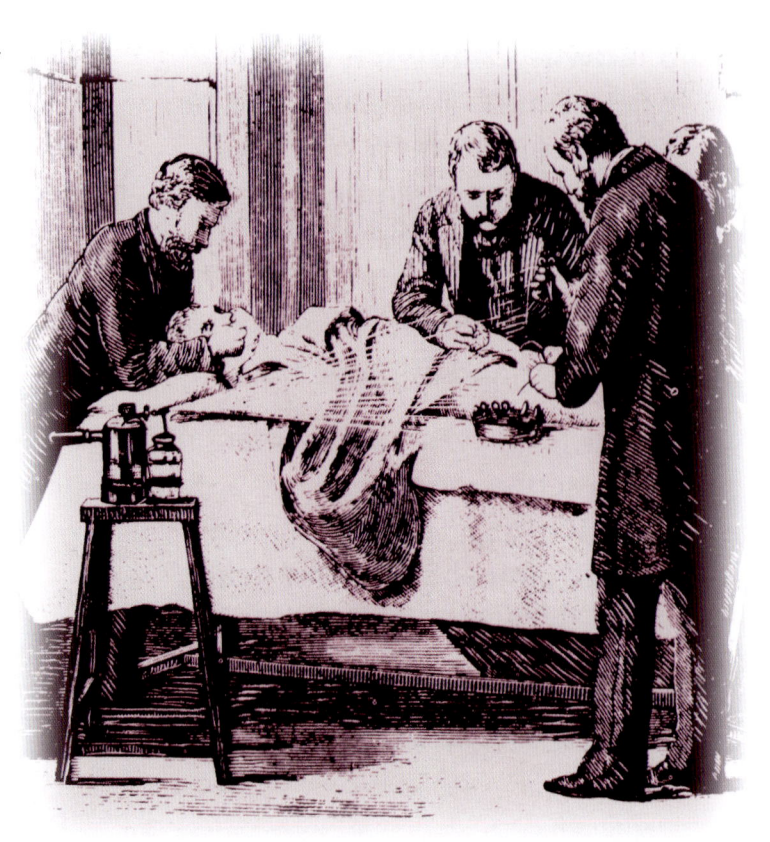

An operation in about 1870. Note the chloroform pad over the man's nose. Even though the doctors are wearing their ordinary clothes and do not wash before the operation, the antiseptic spray kills the germs.

SOURCE G

Thank God for Lister

One of the most feared accidents 100 years ago was a broken arm where the bone came through the skin.   Most people died, or the arm had to be cut off.

When I think of how many of our teenagers break an arm or leg, I give thanks for Joseph Lister.

Written by an American vicar.

Heroes in the Hunt for Health

6. In 1900, 28% of the people in York did not have enough money to live, and 16% did not have enough money to eat.

This made **David Lloyd George** very angry. He set up

- 1908 Old Age pensions
- 1909 Job centres to help people find jobs.
- 1911 Dole money for people who lost their job, and sick pay for people who fell ill.

Ever since Lloyd George, the government has accepted that it is the job of government to take care of the poor people.

A poster from 1911. How is this poster different from Source E on page 67? What is the message of the poster?

THINK ABOUT IT

You have to choose your greatest 'hero of health'. Before you do so, think:

1. Why was the writer of Source F (page 68) thankful for chloroform.
2. Does it help Florence Nightingale that her picture is on a £10 note (page 68)?
3. Does it harm Edwin Chadwick's case that he was sacked (page 69)?
4. Is it fair to say that Pasteur 'discovered' inoculation (page 69)?
5. What is the message of Source G (page 70)?
6. How can Lloyd George be a 'hero of health' when he was not a doctor?

STOP AND REFLECT: For each for the SIX heroes in the hunt for health on pages 68–71:
- Make a list of what they DID.
- Write a sentence to say why they were important.

INVESTIGATING HISTORY

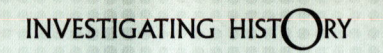

Pulling it Together

Who did most for medicine in the nineteenth century?

In this chapter, you have learned about the people who helped medicine to improve in the nineteenth century.

But who did MOST to help medicine?

Stage 1 Preparation

1. Have a debate: 'Who did most for health before 1910?'

(a) All the pupils choose a favourite 'hero for health' – Nightingale, Simpson, Chadwick, Pasteur, Lister or Lloyd George.

(b) They study their hero's life and think about what their hero did for medicine.

(c) Six pupils volunteer to speak – one for each of the 'heroes'.

(d) The idea is to decide who was the most important. In turn, the six speakers put the case for their hero. When the speakers have finished, the class votes to decide who was the winner.

Stage 2 Writing the webpage

2. Imagine you have been asked to design a webpage for the History department's 'Heroes of Health' website. You must write the webpage about your 'hero for health'.

(a) The page must say:
- What the person did.
- Why what they did was important.
- Why this was the most important improvement in medicine.

(b) Design your webpage with a banner title, a picture, headings and text in different fonts and sizes, and other elements (such as animations and clipart), so that your page will look really good.

(a) The basic webpage *will give facts about the life of the hero for health, and say what they did.*

(b) A better webpage *will explain what the hero did, and say why this was important to medicine.*

(c) A very good webpage *will convince the reader that its hero was vitally important in the history of medicine.*

(d) The best webpage *will prove that its hero was more important than other people who helped medicine improve in the nineteenth century.*

CHAPTER 7

The Empire

Should Britons be proud of the British Empire?

In this chapter you will:
- Learn about how the British Empire grew.
- Study how the British treated the peoples of the Empire.
- Talk about whether the British should pay compensation for the slave trade.
- Study the Irish famine and the Empire in India.
- Write about whether pupils should study the British Empire.

The British people were very proud of the Empire. Maps in school classrooms showed
5 the British Empire coloured red. Children's books were full of the far-off places and peoples that Britain ruled.
10 British people believed that their Empire was good for the world, and that they were taking civilisation 'to peoples
15 who would be **savages** if we did not tell them what to do'.

They never thought that the Empire might be wrong.

In the years after 1945, the countries of the
20 Empire became free. Their historians said that the Empire was a bad thing, which took away their freedom and harmed their way of life.

Was the Empire a good thing, or a bad thing?

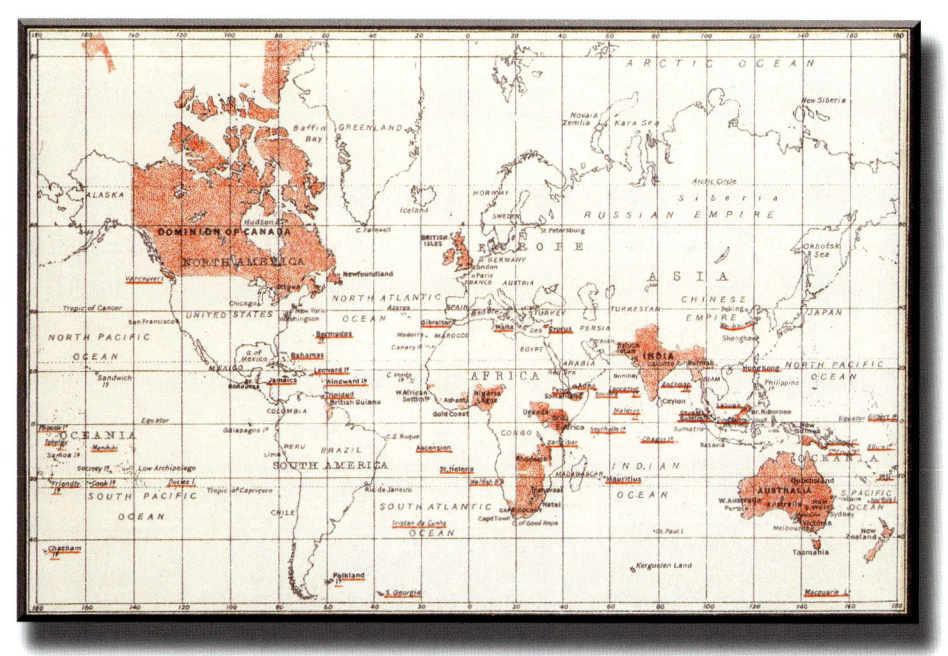

The British Empire in 1905.

> **THINK ABOUT IT**
>
> Is the idea of 'empire' – where one people rules over another – always wrong, or can a well-run empire sometimes be right?

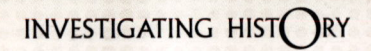

How was the British Empire built?

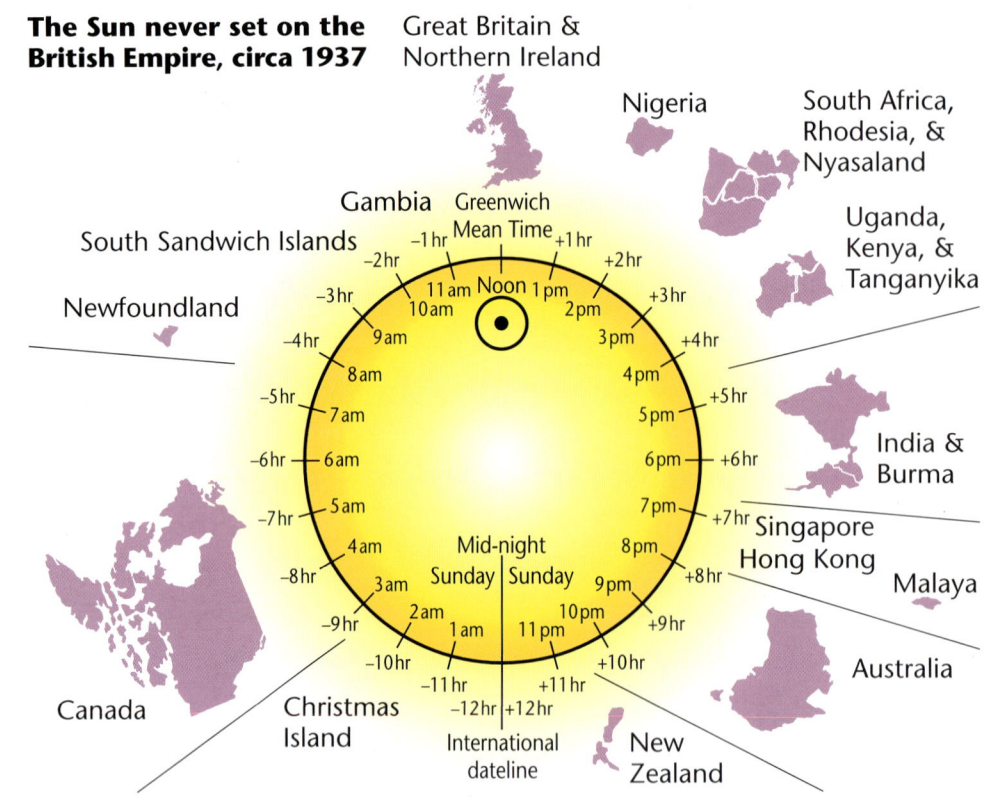

The Sun never set on the British Empire, circa 1937

In 1896 the British Empire covered more than 11 million square miles, with almost 400 million people. The British owned land all over the world – it was 'the Empire on which the sun never set'

The British conquered the Empire bit by bit over 300 years. They ruled different places in different ways. Queen Victoria only called herself the 'Empress' of one country – India.

The First British Empire

Apart from Ireland (which Britain conquered in 1169), the first country to become part of the British Empire was Newfoundland in America in 1585.

The British went to the West Indies to grow sugar, and to North America to grow tobacco. After 1610, the British East India Company set up in India.

French traders went to North America and India too, and France wanted to help their traders do better than the British. In the eighteenth century Britain ended up fighting a war with the French to stop them taking over places that British traders wanted to go. The British won, and ended up with an 'empire' in America and India.

In 1783, the British Empire had a setback – the Americans rebelled and broke free of British rule.

Motives for an Empire

Why did the British build up their Empire?

Some historians say that it was to trade with places, and to stop other countries trading there. Some think the British wanted to take Christianity and civilisation to the 'backward' peoples of the world.

Different British people went overseas for different reasons – for a job, to get land, to have an adventure, or to shoot wild animals.

The British used Australia as a place to send criminals. And they took over Hong Kong so that they could sell drugs in China.

Imperialism

Until 1857, the British government let the East India Company rule India. But in 1857 there was a big revolt in India – the 'Indian Mutiny'. When it ended, the British government took over the government of India.

In the next 25 years the British went empire-mad. They took over 4 million square miles of land – most of it in Africa. The Africans had spears, we had guns.

It is a sad thing that, during this time, the British invented concentration camps – during the war with the Boers in South Africa (1899–1902).

One of Britain's greatest empire builders in Africa was Cecil Rhodes, who wanted Britain to own all of Africa from Egypt to South Africa. When he died, Rhodes left all his money so that even more land could be conquered.

THINK ABOUT IT

1. Choose FIVE important dates in the growth of the British Empire.
2. Find FOUR reasons British people wanted to build up an Empire.

STOP AND REFLECT: Write two sentences about the growth of the British Empire – ONE on something to be proud of, and ONE on something to be ashamed of.

INVESTIGATING HISTORY

What did the British think about the peoples of the Empire?

In the nineteenth century, the writer Rudyard Kipling was very famous in Britain. His most famous book is *Jungle Book*. In the book, the man-cub Mowgli grows up with the animals,
5 but ends up as their ruler because he learns how to control fire.

Jungle Book is more than just a children's story. It is also about evolution – about how man rules over the animals because he is better than
10 the animals.

But Kipling took these ideas further. He believed that – just as man was better than the animals – white men were better than other races. And therefore, he said, white men
15 should rule over them.

Kipling believed that it was the white man's duty to do this, and to bring peace and good government to the world.

THINK ABOUT IT

1. Study the poem in Source A.
   - List some of the nasty things he says about the peoples of the Empire.
   - Look at verse 2. What TWO jobs does he say the White Man should do.
   - Read verse 4. Why, does he say, should the White Man do these things?
2. Is this poem racist? Give TWO reasons for your answer.

SOURCE A

The White Man's Burden

Take up the White Man's burden –
Go out to lands unknown –
Make your sons go help them
The countries that you own;
Make them work and struggle,
For peoples still all wild –
New-conquered, sullen peoples,
Half devil and half child.

Take up the White Man's burden –
Fight wars of peace until –
You feed the poor and hungry,
And cure them if they're ill;
And when you think you've helped them
(And that your battle's won)
Watch stupid, lazy peoples
Wreck everything you've done.

Take up the White Man's burden,
Get what he's always got –
The blame for every problem
Although you've helped a lot –
The hate of those you're taking
(So slowly) to the light:
'Why have you taken from us,
Our lovely backward night?'

Take up the White Man's burden –
Don't do any less –
Don't try to lose the burden
Don't stop a while to rest.
By all you want or wonder,
By all you say or do,
These silent, sullen peoples
Shall judge your God and you.

This poem says the same things as Rudyard Kipling's poem of 1898, only in modern language.

The Empire

SOURCE B

This American cartoon shows a white man carrying a black man to school. Its meaning was that white men were teaching the black peoples how to live properly.

Many people hated Kipling's poem. They said it
20 was **racist**.

One MP wrote an angry poem saying that the British treated the peoples of their Empire very badly (Source C).

> **THINK ABOUT IT**
>
> 1. Study the poem in Source C. Which do you think is the most angry thing it says?
> 2. Study Source B and explain the message of the cartoon. Is the cartoon racist?
> 3. Discuss as a class: if an Empire does good things, but for racist reasons, is it good or evil/right or wrong?

> **STOP AND REFLECT:** Write FIVE bullet points: 'What the British thought about the peoples in their Empire'.

SOURCE C

The Brown Man's Burden

Pile on the brown man's burden
Take, and make them pay;
Go clear away the 'niggers'
If they get in your way;
Be strict with them, for truly,
It's useless to be mild
With conquered, sullen peoples
Half devil and half child.

Pile on the brown man's burden;
And if he starts to hate,
Meet everything he tells you
With ideas up to date.
With guns and shells and bullets
A hundred times made plain
The brown man's loss will give you
What you want again.

Pile on the brown man's burden,
Force him to be fair;
Pretend that all you're doing
You do because you care.
And if, because he's 'stupid'
He questions what you will
Then, in the name of freedom
Pick up your gun and kill.

Written in 1899.

◆ The writer was being sarcastic – really, he hated the way the British treated the peoples of the Empire.

77

Should Britain pay compensation for the slave trade?

SOURCE A

Some people did not agree with the slave trade. This poster shows black people eating and dancing while their white slaves do all the work. Can you see the black slave owner whipping a white slave?

The poster is saying that slavery is wrong. Its message is: 'How would you feel if things were the other way round?'

The Triangular Trade

British people who went to live in America and the West Indies did not have enough people to do
5 the work.

British traders saw a chance to make money. They loaded their ships with guns, wine, cloth, glass and iron – all the things Africans
10 wanted but which were cheap in Britain.

They sailed to Africa and traded them for slaves.

Then they sailed with the slaves to
15 America (this was called 'the Middle Passage'). In America, they traded the slaves for rum, sugar and tobacco.

People in Britain wanted rum,
20 sugar and tobacco, so the traders came back home and sold them for a big profit.

Everybody was happy – except the slaves.

Abolition   25

The British traded slaves for 225 years (1562–1807) and became the greatest slave-trading country in the world. In the ten years from 1795–1804 they   30
took three-quarters of a million Africans to the Americas. It was the biggest mass-movement of people ever in history.

After 1770, William Wilberforce   35
tried to get the slave trade abolished. He was helped by black Africans who had been brought to England (such as Ottobah Cuguano and Olaudah Equiano).   40

They said that slavery was wrong. Their slogan was 'Am I not a Man and a Brother?' They knew lots of terrible facts about the Middle
45 Passage, which made the slave traders look bad, and they used them to turn ordinary people against the slave trade.

In 1807, Parliament abolished the
50 slave trade.

SOURCE B

The Middle Passage – Olaudah Equiano's Story

I was overcome with pain and fear. I fell down and lay on the deck. When I came to, I asked the other people if the white men were going to eat us. They looked so frightening, with their red faces and long hair.

They put me below deck. It was awful. The smell and the crying were terrible. I was seasick and could not eat, but I did not care – all I wanted to do was die.

Down below decks, everybody became ill. It was too hot and airless, and there were so many of us, and we were so overcrowded that we could not even turn over. The fact that we were in chains made things worse.

Only now can I bring myself to tell you the hardships of this evil trade. The screams of the women, and the groans of the dying, made the place so terrible you would not believe it.

The Life of Olaudah Equiano the African (1789).

SOURCE C

The Middle Passage

Never in history has anything so terrible happened to a people as the slave trade. Over 400 years Africans were torn from their homes and sent to the New World. Although we will never know how many people were taken, historians think that between 30 and 60 million Africans were captured by the slave traders and that only a third of them (if that) lived to tell the tale.

From a Slavery website.

THINK ABOUT IT

1. Using Source B, list FIVE bad things about the Middle Passage.

2. Find the value-judgement words used by the writers of Sources B and C, which are trying to influence you to hate the slave trade.

3. Take the role of one of the following: a slave trader, an African slave, or an American planter who needs workers.

   Prepare a short talk to tell the others what *you* think about the slave trade.

The Empire

79

INVESTIGATING HIST**O**RY

In September 2001, the World Conference Against Racism met in South Africa. One of the Africans there said this about the slave trade:

5 'I want this conference to say that the slave trade was a crime against humanity. The countries which did it must say they are sorry, and they should be made to pay money to the countries of Africa.'

10 **Said at the Conference.**

The British government did not agree to the words 'a crime against humanity', and did not want to pay any money. In the end, the Conference did call the slave trade 'a crime against humanity', but it did not ask Britain to pay money for what had happened.

15

If you had been at the Conference, what would you have said?

1. The slave trade took half the people of Africa. It took all the young and strong, and left the old and the sick. It destroyed Africa.

2. Not only the white slave traders carried on the slave trade. The African kings sold the black slaves to them. The African countries ought to say they are sorry for selling the slaves.

3. The slave trade destroyed life for those who it did not take to America. They were always in danger of being made a slave. Many of them stopped trying to work, and sold their children to be slaves.

4. What was so good about Africa *before* the slave trade? It was poor, and the African kings were bad men. One American slave said she was glad to go to America.

5. The slave trade destroyed the countries of Africa. Afterwards, it was only a matter of time before Britain conquered them.

6. The slave trade only affected a small part of West Africa. Everything else went on as normal.

7. Slavery is WRONG. There is no more to say.

80

The Empire

8. You cannot blame the British for being slave traders when NO ONE at the time – not even the Africans – thought it was wrong.

9. The slave trade not only harmed the slaves, it harmed the slave traders too – it turned them into animals.

10. Other countries – France, Denmark, Portugal, Spain – traded slaves. Britain gave up the slave trade in 1807 and spent the next 100 years trying to STOP it!

11. You cannot punish modern British people for something that happened hundreds of years ago and which they would not do today.

12. The stories about the Middle Passage were told by Wilberforce and his friends, so they made it sound much worse than it was. No more people died on the slave ships than did on other ships, and the slave traders tried to look after the slaves – they wanted to sell them, not let them die!

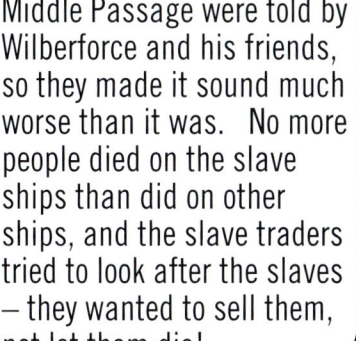

Slaves rescued by a British warship, 1870.

13. Slavery was racist – white people captured and sold black Africans.

14. The slave trade made Britain rich by robbing Africa.

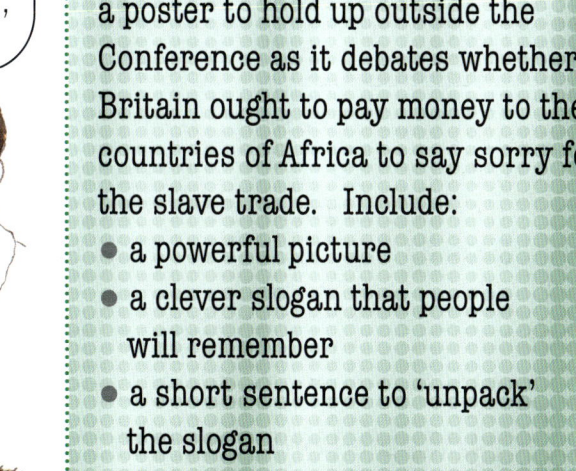

THINK ABOUT IT

1. Split the statements into two piles – those which might have been said by British people at the Conference Against Racism, and those that might have been said by Africans.

2. Hold your own 'Slave Trade Conference'. Ask your teacher to act as chairperson. Debate whether – and how – Britain should make amends for the slave trade.

STOP AND REFLECT: Using ICT, design a poster to hold up outside the Conference as it debates whether Britain ought to pay money to the countries of Africa to say sorry for the slave trade. Include:
- a powerful picture
- a clever slogan that people will remember
- a short sentence to 'unpack' the slogan
- different types and sizes of font to make the poster look good.

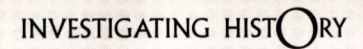

The Great Hunger – Research Study 1

England conquered Ireland in 1169. After 1801, Britain ruled Ireland from London.

The Catholic people of Ireland were poor. Many of them lived on nothing but potatoes. In 1845, a potato disease from America destroyed the potato crop. The same thing happened in 1846, 1847 and 1848.

There was a **famine**. Many Irish people starved to death.

The British response

Most British people did nothing. Some were glad that the Catholics were dying. Some English people blamed the Irish – they said that they were drunken and lazy and that it served them right.

Also, at the time, people believed that governments should not do anything about things like famine. They asked the government to leave the Irish to help themselves.

In fact, the government *did* do something. It set up soup kitchens and gave Irish people jobs building roads. It gave £7 million to help, a vast sum for the times. It was not enough. The Irish people still starved to death.

The Empire

FACT FILE

Ireland's problems before 1845

- The population was growing quickly.
- Many Irish farms were tiny. They were too small to keep a family at the best of times.
- Most of the land in Ireland was owned by English people who did not care about it or the Irish.
- The potatoes. A tiny farm growing potatoes could feed a family of eight, and all the farmer needed was a spade. By 1845, many Irish lived on nothing but potatoes.

SOURCE A

One million people died in what was at that time the richest country in the world. This still causes pain today. The English stood by and let a potato disease turn into a human disaster.

Tony Blair (1997).

Aftermath

One million people starved. 1½ million more went to America. Disease followed hunger. It was a terrible time.

Many Irish blame the English for the famine – they say that the English tried to kill all the Irish. In 1997, Prime Minister Tony Blair said he was sorry for the famine (Source A).

THINK ABOUT IT

1. Find some facts on page 83 to show that the Irish famine still affects people today.
2. Why are many Americans so interested in the famine?

In 1998 the Irish living in the American town of Boston put up this statue to remember the famine. Schoolteachers in New York are told to teach their pupils that the English government's actions during the famine were as bad as the Nazi attempt to kill all the Jews.

83

SOURCE B

If the Irish think we will give them money, they will all become beggars... It is not the job of the government to give people food...

God sent this disaster to teach the Irish a lesson, to show them what happens when you are lazy, troublesome and violent.

The English head of Famine Aid.

SOURCE C

God sent the potato disease, but the English made the famine. 1½ million people were carefully killed, on purpose, by the English government.

During these years, Ireland was growing enough food to feed everybody, but the English were selling it. For every food ship that went to Ireland to help the starving, six ships left to feed the English.

John Mitchel, writing in 1873.

SOURCE D

Wheat imports and exports to Ireland ('000 tons)

	Exports	Imports	Net
1844	424	30	+394
1845	513	28	+485
1846	284	197	+87
1847	146	889	-743
1848	314	439	-125

John Mitchel said that more food left Ireland than was sent to Ireland during the famine. Do these figures support what he said?

SOURCE E

The government never tried to stop food going to Ireland. The government did not force the Irish to export their food. Irish farmers chose to sell their food to the English.

An Irish website.

SOURCE F

This English cartoon shows Ireland as a bad baby wanting more and more.

SOURCE G

Nobody is saying that the English caused the famine. But, because they did not care, they let the Irish die... Ireland was destroyed by the most powerful country in the world, which wanted to conquer it, steal from it and make its people slaves.

Written by the modern historian Mark Thornton.

SOURCE H

Although the Irish *say* the English were to blame for the famine, the papers of the time show that lots of English were kind and good people who tried very hard to help. There was no plot to kill all the Irish.

Jennifer Payne, a modern English historian.

SOURCE I

In 1995 the Irish Parliament talked about the Great Famine. This is what three people said:

- Mr M McDowell: Many Irish people of the time did not go hungry, and did not care about the Irish people who were dying. They were no different from the English people of the time, who just did not know what was going on.

- Mr Andrew: I have read a lot about this during the summer, and I think it is wrong when people say we should forgive the English for something that happened 150 years ago. I cannot forgive them. They were to blame.

- Mr Connor: I do not think the English government tried to kill the Irish. There were famines in England at this time, and the government ignored them too, and left the people to die. That is what they were like in those days. They thought it was not the government's job to feed people.

SOURCE J

If we are going to judge the way the English government handled the famine, we need to know three things:

- What did it do?
- Why did it do these things?
- Was it successful?

The modern historian Paul Thompson, writing in 1996.

THINK ABOUT IT

1. Study Sources B–I, then discuss as a class:

   a. Were the English to blame for the famine?

   b. Did the English government *try* to kill the Irish people?

   c. Can English people be proud of the way the English government handled the famine?

   d. Were the English government's actions during the famine as bad as the Nazi attempt to kill all the Jews?

2. Will it affect people's opinion of the famine if they are English or Irish?

STOP AND REFLECT: Write as much as you can to finish this sentence: 'I think/ do not think that Tony Blair should have said he was sorry for the famine because…'

INVESTIGATING HISTORY

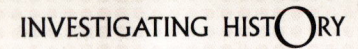

The British Rule in India – Research Study 2

SOURCE A

Every summer, the British moved the whole government 1000 miles from Calcutta to the hill town of Simla, where the weather was cooler. This photo shows the Post Office at Simla, and the postmen with their wagon. The drivers said that they were the best postmen in the world, and got the post through storm and snow, disaster and danger.

SOURCE B

The Indian Civil Service

The Indian **Civil Service** was the best, most honest government man has ever had. A story shows this. A young British man ran out of money and borrowed £50 from an Indian, giving the Indian an IOU written on a bit of paper. A year later, the IOU came back to the young man with the marks of many people on it. Dozens of people all over Asia had used it as money, knowing it could be trusted.

Written by a modern historian.

Queen Victoria was 'Empress of India'. The British were very proud of their rule in India (they called it 'the **raj**').

So here is the British Empire at its best. Study pages 86–90, making a note of all the good things you can find about the British rule in India – and also any bad things you find.

Was the British government of India of a high quality?

SOURCE C

British India

The raj was a bluff. Some 300 million Indians were ruled by 1500 men of the Indian Civil Service and a few soldiers. If the Indians had wanted to throw out the British, they could have done so.

Written by a modern historian.

SOURCE D

Good Works

British brains, British trade and British money changed India. Many bridges, 40,000 miles of railway, and 70,000 miles of roads show how hard the British worked. They brought water to vast areas of farmland. They built sewers, gave good wages, built canals and handed out food. As a result, famines almost ended.

Written in 1932 by a British person who had lived in India.

The Empire

SOURCE E

Government spending 1913–14

Administration (ICS)	27%
Armed forces	25%
Education	4%
Medical/public health	2%
Railways/irrigation/roads	17%
Other	25%

SOURCE F

British Interests

The British only did things that would help them back in Britain. They built railways to get goods back to Britain.

Written by an Indian professor.

SOURCE G

Many of the things that the Indians grew were for British factories. This shows Indians sorting Indigo to send to Britain.

SOURCE H

Care and Famine

We do not care for the people of India. We do not care enough to stop them dying slow and terrible deaths from things we could easily stop.

We have taken their land, and we rule it, for our good not theirs. And for their lives and deaths we do not care.

Written by Florence Nightingale in 1878.

◆ In 1877 there was a famine, followed by disease. Six million Indians died. The government sent food ships from London, but they were little help.

THINK ABOUT IT

Read Sources A–H.

1. List every example of good government you can find.

2. Find some facts to suggest that the British were only looking after their own interests.

3. Discuss with a friend: Were the British good rulers of India?

INVESTIGATING HISTORY

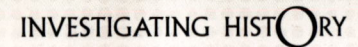

Was Lord Curzon a good Viceroy of India, 1899–1905?

SOURCE I

This photo shows Lord Curzon with a rich Indian.

- Curzon went to Oxford University. He worked 14 hours a day. He did lots of good works in India – he built lots of schools and rebuilt many old Indian buildings.
- He believed that the British Empire was 'the best thing for humankind in the history of the world'.
- What does this photo suggest about the way he treated the Indians?

SOURCE J

Duty

Fight for the right. Hate wrong. Do not worry what others say about you – good or bad. Always be brave. Never give up.

This is how Lord Curzon said in 1905 that he had tried to do his job in India.

SOURCE K

Curzon and the Army

Some drunks from the army killed an Indian, and the unit tried to hush it up. They were rich young men with powerful fathers back home, and they let it be known that they would harm Curzon if he tried to do anything.

Curzon had every man called back to his unit, stopped all leave for the next six months, and punished the regiment very strictly.

'Do not tell me that an Indian's life does not matter… I have set my face like stone against such an evil,' wrote Curzon.

Nobody ever attacked an Indian again.

Written by a modern historian.

The Empire

SOURCE L

Curzon's Durbar, 1903
A durbar was a great meeting. When Edward VII became King, Curzon held a great durbar. The meeting ground was so big that they had to build a railway, five miles long, to take people round it. There was a huge tent showing how great India had been. The durbar went on for ten days, and finished with a Christian church service. At night there were balls and feasts.

On New Year's Day, a million people watched thousands of princes, soldiers and elephants march past Lord and Lady Curzon.

THINK ABOUT IT

Using Sources I–L:

- Find something Curzon did of which British people can be proud.
- Is there anything he did that was not so good?

Was Curzon a good ruler of India?

Were the British in India racist?

SOURCE M

Arrogance

An old Indian once told me that it seemed to him that most Englishmen walk round as though God wanted all the world to be English.

Written by an Oxford University professor in 1875.

SOURCE N

Indians in the Indian Civil Service

There was nothing on paper to stop an Indian going into the Indian Civil Service, but to do so he had to go to university in England and do the exams in London. It cost £1000. Out of 1500 people in the Indian Civil Service, only 50 were Indians.

Written in 1952 by a British person who had been to India.

SOURCE O

In India, but not part of it

We were looked after by Indian servants, and met many Indians, but once you went into your house you were back in Britain. We made our homes as English as we could.

I can't really say I learned very much from India.

The wife of an Englishman in the Indian Civil Service.

SOURCE P

A British family with their Indian servants.

SOURCE Q

Class not Race

The British were not racist. They were much more worried about class. A lord in the Indian Civil Service would feel much closer to a rich Indian than he would to a middle-class Englishman.

Written by a modern historian.

THINK ABOUT IT

Study sources M–Q – were the British in India racist?

STOP AND REFLECT: Write a sentence to answer the question: 'Was British rule in India good?'

The Empire

Pulling it Together

Should Britons be proud of the British Empire?

From an Internet Forum

>> I now firmly believe the British Empire was the kindest and the best Empire ever – and I am very proud to be British today because of it. The Empire helped people and it was not racist.
Paulie (2002)

>> Why is it wrong for Nazi 2 take over Europe, but not wrong 4 Brits to take over the world? Shame!
Questioner (2002)

Since 1988, the government has told teachers what subjects they must study. But when it came to History, there was a big argument about whether pupils ought to study the British Empire. Some people said it was an important part of Britain's past. Some said it ought to be forgotten.

You are going to have your say in that argument.

Stage 1 Preparation

1. Look back over pages 73–91 with a friend. Make two lists:
- one of all the bad things about the British Empire
- one of all the good things.

2. As a class, share your ideas, and then have a class debate: 'Should Britons be proud of the British Empire?'

3. Decide if you think pupils should study the British Empire.

Stage 2 Writing the letter

4. Imagine you are your parent. Write a letter to your headteacher saying why you want/do not want your child to have to study the British Empire in History.

(a) A basic letter *will list some good things and/or some bad things about the British Empire.*

(b) A better letter *will say whether pupils ought to study the British Empire. It will give a reason why this should be so, and will give some facts about the Empire.*

(c) A very good letter *will give a number of reasons why pupils should/ should not study the British Empire, backing up its argument with facts.*

(d) The best letter *will say that pupils must study good and bad things in history.*

POSTSCRIPT
What did Jack the Ripper ever do for us?

> Men will look back and say that I was the start of the twentieth century.
>
> *Jack the Ripper in the film* From Hell, *2001.*

The modern film *From Hell* brings the story of Jack the Ripper to the modern film-goer.

But it does not tell the true story of the Jack the Ripper of 1888.

In the modern film:

- The girls are friends. They are killed because they know that the Queen's grandson has married an ordinary girl.
- Queen Victoria knows about the murders.
- The murders are done by Dr William Gull, the Queen's doctor. He is mad and thinks he is equal to God.
- In all the murders, the murderer cuts open the body.
- Whitechapel is shown as a very poor place.
- Fred Abberline is shown as a drug addict. Although he finds out the truth, there is a 'cover-up' to stop him making it public.
- Abberline falls in love with Mary Kelly. She gets away, and goes to live at the seaside.

When we looked at the Ripper story on pages 4–6, we saw that the story could never have happened in 1688. But the Ripper also could never have done what he did in the modern film.

A modern film called From Hell *has been made about Jack the Ripper.*

THINK ABOUT IT

Compare the true story of Jack the Ripper (pages 4–6) with the film.

(a) What bits of the film are true?

(b) What facts does the film leave out?

(c) What facts does the film make up to add to the true story?

(d) Suggest why it does this.

Postscript

> **FACT FILE**
>
> **The Washington sniper – a modern serial killer**
>
> In October 2002, a **serial killer** started killing people in America.
>
> - He shot 10 people and wounded three others using a rifle.
> - The killings were drive-by shootings of people he did not know (e.g. a woman shopper).
> - The shootings happened all over the north east of the United States.
> - There was lots of interest on TV about the killings.
> - Police did not know who was doing the killings.
> - The killer was captured when police found a fingerprint from an earlier crime. A call was put out over the radio, and a passer-by saw the killer's car.
> - The killer was an ex-soldier. He had become a Muslim in 1985 and wanted to destroy America. He had a history of mental illness.
> - Some people blamed America – where many people are so poor.

THINK ABOUT IT

1. Compare the true story of Jack the Ripper (on pages 4–6) with the story of the Washington sniper.

   a) How are the stories the same?

   b) What is different?

   c) Why did American police catch the sniper, but London police could not catch the Ripper?

2. How does the story of the Washington sniper help us to understand what has – and what has not – changed since 1888? Think about:
   - science
   - living conditions
   - religion
   - public opinion
   - what people think about foreigners.

> **STOP AND REFLECT:** Why are we so interested in the story of Jack the Ripper today?

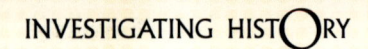

GLOSSARY

abolition/abolish To do away with/ to bring to an end (e.g. the slave trade).

almshouses In the nineteenth century, houses provided free of rent for old people.

antiseptic A chemical that kills germs.

ballot A vote in an election made in secret and put into a 'ballot box'.

biased Tending to support only one side of the argument – misrepresenting the facts to support that side.

British Empire Lands overseas conquered by Britain and ruled by the British.

cannibalism Where one human being eats another.

Chartists People who tried to get the government to accept a 'Charter' (petition) which would give ordinary people political rights.

Civil Service The government officials who run the administration of the government – as opposed to the MPs, who make the laws that the Civil Service have to administer.

civilisation The way a people/society lives, especially all its finer beliefs and achievements.

Communism/Communists The belief that no person has the right to own land or a factory, and that factories make 'wage-slaves' of the workers.

constituency An area/place that elects a single MP to Parliament.

democracy Government by the people – usually by voting for their government.

dole Unemployment pay.

durbar An Indian word, meaning a state ceremony held by a ruler.

election The time when people in a democracy vote for the government they want.

evolution The belief that humankind developed slowly from single-cell creatures over millions of years – the opposite of 'creation' which believes that God made the world.

famine Where large numbers of people die of hunger.

freedom of speech The right, in Britain, to criticise the government.

hymn A religious song sung in worship.

Industrial Revolution 'Industry' is the way people make things. A revolution is a complete change-around from the past – in industry, society or politics – often violent. So the Industrial Revolution was a complete change in the way things were made.

inoculation Giving a dead or weakened form of a germ to a person, so that the person is able to build up immunity to that illness.

midden muck-heap

missionaries People of a certain religion who go to another country to try to make converts.

oath When you swear something (e.g. on the Bible).

overlookers People employed to keep the workers working as hard as possible.

pension Payment of income to an old person who has stopped work.

picket When Trade Unionists stand outside a factory during a strike, and try to persuade other workers there to go on strike too.

privy toilet

pocket boroughs A borough was a place that elected an MP. Pocket boroughs had only one voter, which allowed corruption.

pollution Damage of any kind to the environment – air, water or land.

Prime Minister The leader of the biggest political Party in Parliament – leader of the government.

prostitute A woman who gives sex for money.

Public Health Measures taken by the government to give people a clean water supply, sewerage, healthy food, etc.

racist/racism The hatred/criticism of another group of people solely because of their race, racial traditions and the colour of their skin.

raj An Indian word, meaning 'rule', applied to the British Empire in India.

Glossary

reform When the government passes a law to change something for the better.

revival A sudden growth in enthusiasm for religion.

rotten boroughs A borough was a place which elected an MP. Rotten boroughs had very few voters, which allowed corruption.

Salvation Army 'Salvation' is the religious experience when Christians believe that Jesus Christ has saved them from going to Hell. The Salvation Army believed they were fighting against evil in a battle for the souls of men.

savages A hate-word for people who have not achieved as high a level of civilisation as you think you have.

Science/scientific The systematic study of nature to find how it works.

serial killer A murderer who kills more than two victims.

slum An area of very poor housing.

suffragettes Women who used violence to try to get the vote for women.

Trade Unions Unions of workers, set up to get better conditions and wages for their members.

workhouse Building where poor people were sent if they wanted poor relief.

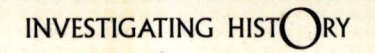

INDEX

Ballot Act 57

Chartism 54, 61
coal 10

doctors 66–67
durbar 89

Empire 8, 73–90
factories 19, 20, 22, 23–31, 33

Great Exhibition 16–17

India 86–90
Irish Famine 82–85
iron 10, 21

Labour Party 54, 58
London 4–6, 35–41

match-girls' strike 33
medicine 30, 65–70
missionaries 50–51

Newgate Prison 40

Parliament 53–63, 79
pensions 20, 30, 57, 71
people
    Besant, Annie 33
    Booth, William 48–49
    Brunel, Isambard Kingdom 14–15
    Carey, William 51
    Chadwick, Edwin 69
    Curzon, Lord 88–89
    Darby, Abraham 10, 11
    Darwin, Charles 46, 47
    Dickens, Charles 35–37
    Engels, Frederick 19, 28, 46
    George I 54, 55
    Hunt, Holman 44
    Jack the Ripper 4–6, 92
    Kipling, Rudyard 76–77
    Lister, Joseph 70
    Livingstone, David 50–51
    Lloyd George, David 71
    Loveless, George 32
    Merrick, John (the Elephant Man) 9
    Nightingale, Florence 15, 68, 87
    Oastler, Richard 24
    Pankhurst, Emmeline 62
    Pasteur, Louis 69
    Rhodes, Cecil 75
    Sadler, Michael 24, 27–28
    Salt, Titus 30–31
    Shaftesbury, Lord 28
    Simpson, James 68
    Slessor, Mary 51
    Studd, C T 51
    Taylor, James Hudson 51
    Victoria, Queen 6, 16, 53, 74, 86, 92
    Wilberforce, William 55, 78, 81
    Wilkes, John 54, 55
Peterloo 54, 60
police 4–6, 92–93
pollution 21–23
poor 4, 6, 20, 35, 36, 40, 48–49, 71

racism 6, 17, 76–77, 90
railways 12–13, 14
Reform Acts 54, 56, 57
religion 31, 43–51, 82

Saltaire 30–31
Salvation Army 48–49
sick pay 20, 57, 71
slave trade 51, 55, 78–81
Suffragettes 54, 62–63
sutee 51

textiles 11, 19, 24–29, 30–31
Tolpuddle Martyrs 32
trade unions 20, 32–33

workhouse 40